WALK IN POWER

Equipping the Saints for Ministry
Personal Testimonies and Real-life Experiences

Lenn Olivarez

LEANDRO OLIVAREZ

© Copyright 2023 Leandro Olivarez

All rights reserved. No part of this collection may be reproduced or transmitted in any form or by any means, electronic or mechanical, including photocopying and recording, or by any information storage and retrieval system, except in the case of brief quotations for use in articles and reviews, without written permission from the author.

7710-T Cherry Park Dr, Ste 224

Houston, TX 77095

(713)-766-4271

ISBN: 978-0-9997837-6-4

In Loving Memory
Of My Nephew,
Tai Nguyen

I would like to take this opportunity to acknowledge my amazing nephew, Tai:

Tai, I know that you are busy right now, singing awesome praises to our Lord. I also understand that you may or may not be aware of what I am writing to you right now; however, I believe that the Lord will call your name and summon you to His throne to hear this.

Tai, we all love you and miss you immensely. I want you to know that the one thing that gives us all comfort is knowing that you are in heaven with our Savior, Jesus Christ. I felt so helpless standing at the window of your hospital room. I know the Holy Spirit was there with us and stayed with you until it was time to escort you to heaven. I am thankful that we made eye contact and prayed together through the glass. I was blessed when you called me just before you went into the hospital and said these words to me: "Uncle Lenn, I want you to know that I have been listening to your preaching, and I gave my life to Jesus Christ, I am saved!" Glory to God!

As much comfort as it brings, life without you just isn't the same. We have all taken your passing hard, but you must know that Cindi and the kids have been up to some amazing things. You'd be so proud of them. Your household has been looked after by the very ones that held you up in prayer through your battle.

Everyone misses you like crazy. Grandma and Grandpa think about you often. Even my little one remembers our boat ride with you on the 4th of July 2021. I still have my light-up suit you made us men wear a few Christmases ago. I will always cherish our time together and our Disney trip to Florida. Such great memories with Maxson, Nguyen, and the Olivarez bunch. We miss you tremendously.

You did an excellent job as a husband and daddy, brother to Reed and Tracie, and uncle to all the kids. You were an awesome grandson to Grandpa and Grandma Olivarez, a wonderful son to Tony and Sue, and an amazing nephew to Shawni, Rick, Grace, Steven, Gloria, Priscilla, and me. We feel honored to have called you "ours".

Tai, my wife, and kids love you, and I look forward to that crawfish boil in heaven.

Until we see each other again in the Lord's kingdom.

Love,

Uncle Lenn and family

Dedication

To Priscilla, my beautiful wife, my very best friend. I knew that God had the right woman for me the day I met you. I am a blessed man. God has blessed me beyond measure through you. In you, I find purpose, encouragement, and the desire to be the man that you deserve, the man that God intended me to be. Thank you for being strong in faith and always ready to support my decision and stand by my side as my best friend, life companion, and spiritual warrior. I look forward to growing old with you. I love you.

To My Beautiful Children, Jacob, Alison, Linden, and Liam, I always knew that God had someone special just for me. I knew that one day he would give me someone so special that no one in this whole world would have. Someone set aside just for me. Then, one by one, God graced me with you, my beautiful children. I don't have the words to even tell you how much I love each of you. You make me want to be a better man and a better dad for you all, God will bless each one of you greatly, you will all be prosperous, happy, joyful, smart, and strong, and you will have the favor of God over you and your seed. The Lord will be the heartbeat of your lives. Always trust in Jesus Christ. Always remember, you are never alone; I love you forever and always.

My Pastors, My Mentors, My Parents

I don't even think words in any language even exist to express my deepest gratitude to my beautiful, amazing parents, who also happen to be my senior pastors, as well as my spiritual mentors, Mr. and Mrs. Vivian and Lucia Olivarez.

I could never thank you enough for the love you have given me and my wife and children. You have been the perfect example of true leaders that anyone could ever ask for. You have taught so many and loved us all unconditionally. My prayer is for the Lord to guard and watch over you both for many more years. Giving you a double portion of the Lord's grace and peace. You have faithfully served in the ministry for over 37 years. I pray that I will be granted a double portion of the Holy Spirit anointing that the Lord has graced you with.

Mom and Dad, I love you more than I could ever express. Thank you from the bottom of my heart.

To My Amazing Family

God has given me the most supportive family that anyone could ever ask for. Without you all, I don't think we could have survived the way we have. You each have an amazing story to tell that would absolutely change lives. Sulema and Tony Moreno, Shawni Alexander, Steven and Gloria Olivarez, and Grace and Rick James; You have been the most supportive brothers and sisters that Priscilla and I could ever ask for. I love you with all my heart and thank you for your priceless contribution to the world as follows; Tai (RIP) and Lucinda Nguyen, Lauren and Shelby, Tracy and Reed Maxson, Ethen and Kaitlyn, The Olivarez Bunch Steven, Nathan, Johnathan, Nicolas, Marianna, and Kylie James. I believe in each one of you. May the Lord protect and guide you all forever.

To My Awesome Church Family,

To all the families of Templo de Alabanza "Temple of Praise," located in Rockport, Texas.

I want you all to know that my family and I love each of you with all our hearts. I am so very happy to be a part of your life and your children's lives. I am so excited for your growth in Christ. You have all become true warriors and generals for the Lord in the battle we call life. Always remember, you are never alone. Never give up, stay strong in the power of His might, and put on the full armor of God daily.

It has been an honor for me to serve you and your beautiful families, pray with you, worship side by side with you, and to even go into battle with many of you. I am honored to call you my brothers and sisters. Always remember to make the devil regret messing with you and your family. There are a few of you I want to acknowledge for playing a major role in my spiritual growth as a pastor and as a servant of God. I am your brother and friend for life.

Priscilla Olivarez, James "Bubba" Poiner, Tony and Sulema Moreno, Dennis Chupe, Shawni Alexander, Rick and Grace James, Steven and Gloria Olivarez, Cantu Family, Cherry Morrill, Juanita Mora, Jesus and Lucy Cerda.

I love you all, blessings into eternity!

Pastor Lenn

LEANDRO OLIVAREZ

Foreword

Pastor Lenn Olivarez, has been on the front lines of Spiritual Warfare since 2010.

He has ministered deliverance to the oppressed and engaged in the front-line battles to set the captives free. Since Pastor Lenn's first book, *A New Life Is Expecting You*, reached many souls for Christ around the world with powerful testimonies of how God can transform the life of anyone willing to allow Him to set them free, and set them on a new course of purpose in life.

The vision for this book is to arm the body of Christ. We see too many of our brothers and sisters in the church living defeated lives. We as the Church need to stop and ask ourselves, why? This is not the life of the redeemed. Why are there believers in Jesus who are still addicted to pornography, alcohol, and drugs? Why is there so much abuse in many believers' homes? Why are Christians dying of illnesses, and the people of God giving up and committing suicide?

The reason all of this is happening is that Jesus Christ is too often left out of the Church. Many in the Church today know very little, if anything, about the person and work of the Holy Spirit. Our mission is to expose the enemy and arm the church by showing the Scriptures and building faith in the hearts and minds of every believer.

We are to stand on the living Word of God that says, "You are more than a conqueror, and by His stripes, we are healed." The enemy has infiltrated the Church, and since we are truly living in the last days, it is time for the sleeping giant called the Church of the One True Living God to arise and invade the enemy's camp. The Lord has given the Church authority over all the power of the enemy.

(Luke 10:19) That includes the evil spirits ruling over our nation, our counties, our schools, and our governments. Why is prayer the last thing the Church does when it should be our lifestyle, praying to see the Kingdom of God dismantle the plans of evil? We, the Church, must make this personal, as prayer is who we are and not what we do. Prayer should be as natural as breathing to those of us who love our Lord Jesus Christ.

May the Lord bless you and arm you with His Holy Spirit and fire as you open the pages of this book. Our prayers are blessings upon you and your home and your children, and children's children. You are about to read real-life accounts of how God speaks to His people and instructs us daily on how to pray and learn firsthand; how He wants to use you for His honor and glory and show you your true weapons of spiritual warfare; and how to break down the enemy by exposing the enemy's plans of attack against you and your family.

Ask the Lord right now, before you turn this page, to open your spiritual understanding and to cover you with His precious blood, and for Him to speak to your purpose. God bless you friend; we will see you on the inside.

Contents

INTRODUCTION 1

CHAPTER 1 3
    ANSWER THE CALL

CHAPTER 2 17
    CALLED INTO ACTION

CHAPTER 3 29
    DESTINATION HEAVEN

CHAPTER 4 37
    INNER PRISON

CHAPTER 5 49
    OVERCOMING DEPRESSION

CHAPTER 6 65
    THE REAL YOU

CHAPTER 7 75
    POWER

CHAPTER 8 83
    DECREE AND DECLARE

CHAPTER 9 91
    CASTING ALL YOUR CARES

CHAPTER 10 105
    TIME TO LIVE

CHAPTER 11 117
    GENERAL OF WAR

CHAPTER 12 123
    INSTRUCTIONS FOR BATTLE

CHAPTER 13 .... **135**
  SERPENTS AND SCORPIONS
CHAPTER 14 .... **145**
  LETTING GO OF THE PAST
CHAPTER 15 .... **159**
  "LOVE"
CHAPTER 16 .... **171**
  PRAYERS
CONCLUSION **179**

Introduction

My name is Leandro "Lenn" Olivarez, I am the pastor of a non-denominational church in Rockport, Texas, Templo De Alabanza "Temple of Praise." What you are about to read are personal testimonies and real-life experiences. There is no speculation involved. It has all been lived by either myself or my senior pastors, who are also my parents Mr. and Mrs. Vivian and Lucia Olivarez. You may have read their awesome testimonies in my first book, *A New Life Is Expecting You*. This book is a spinoff of that book with the purpose of building your faith and confidence, knowing that you are a child of the one true Living God and your worth through Christ.

We believe in the full power of Jesus Christ. From the gifts of the Holy Spirit, binding and loosing, spiritual warfare, salvation, the power of the blood of Jesus, and His Second Coming.

The stories that you are about to read are meant to give God all the honor and Glory and to speak to your spirit. They are to let you know that there is no problem bigger than our God. You will see God's words come to life and be able to compare my experiences with your own. The power of God is available to every believer of Jesus Christ so we will not live defeated in any area of our lives.

I pray that you will come into this with an open mind and heart and receive a huge blessing and a new direction from God through this book. You may have been through some hard, heartbreaking times. I am not here to knock you down. I feel that everything that I have experienced was meant for this very moment. May the Lord use my stories to help guide you to the feet of Jesus so that you can touch the tip of His robe and be made whole. God has so much more for you and your loved ones.

Remember. You are loved by our Lord Jesus. I hope you will pick up a copy of my first book, *A New Life Is Expecting You*. I have been in the ministry for more than thirty-seven years, led by the Holy Spirit. I've experienced much, and the Lord has never left my side. I'm here to walk with you step-by-step through this new journey.

Allow me to pray for you.

> *Heavenly Father, I come to you in the name of Jesus Christ, your Son, my savior. I ask you to multiply grace, favor, and blessings for the person reading this book. Give them supernatural wisdom and open their spiritual understanding to see what you want them to see.*
>
> *Lord, I apply the precious blood of Jesus over my reader. May your Holy Spirit fill them with new hope, with encouragement, as well as anoint them with a new vision. Speak to them, Lord. Breathe into their soul and revive their spirit. In Jesus' name, I pray, Amen.*

Chapter 1

Answer the Call

Many people want more of God but don't know where or how to start. Be assured, you do have a calling from God. Please understand that I am not suggesting you do it my way. However, I will share with you the steps I took, after many years, of trying to find a way to break down mental and emotional walls that were keeping me from experiencing His glory in my walk with the Lord. Let's not forget that God tells us the harvest fields are ready, but the laborers are few. The harvest fields are people all over the world who are longing for something real, but don't know what they are looking for, or where to find it. Yes, indeed, you most certainly do have a calling from God. Understand, the moment you accepted Jesus Christ as your Lord and Savior, He deposited in you, His Spirit. His Holy Spirit is all you will ever need to fulfill His purposes for your life.

The Holy Spirit brings gifts with Him. These gifts are the fire of His character. In the book of Luke, John the Baptist tells us a little bit about Jesus and the gift of The Holy Spirit.

> Luke 3:16 - John answered, saying to all, "I indeed baptize you with water; but one mightier than I is coming, whose sandal strap I am not worthy to loose. He will baptize you with the Holy Spirit and fire."

Please allow me to give you a better understanding of His "fire". This is the very fire that makes demons run. This fire is the powerful anointing of the Holy Spirit expressed through His gifts. There are nine of them.

> 1 Corinthians 12:7-11: But the manifestation of the Spirit is given to each one for the profit of all: for to one is given the word of wisdom through the Spirit, to another the word of knowledge through the same Spirit, to another faith by the same Spirit, to another gift of healings by [a] the same Spirit, to another the working of miracles, to another prophecy, to another discerning of spirits, to another different kind of tongues, to another the interpretation of tongues. But one and the same Spirit works all these things, distributing to each one individually as He wills.

Today's Church sees too little of the baptism of the Holy Spirit, which is the anointing of the Holy Spirit, the spiritual fire that flows through the Lord's church as He intended. When we are plugged into The Holy Spirit, we then bare His Character which is the fruit of The Spirit.

> Galatians 5:22, 23 - But the fruit of the Spirit is love, joy, peace, long-suffering, kindness, goodness, faithfulness, gentleness, self-control. Against such there is no law.

We have the honor of not only walking with the Lord, but seeing His Holy Spirit manifest His character in us. This is how we can do all things through Christ, realizing Christ in us is the hope of glory.

Then we have that shallow person who is always around that will spew their inexperienced opinion and will not listen to a preacher or a bible teacher if he doesn't have a theology degree. They say that we are "self-appointed" ministers. I don't know about you, but I don't think one needs a college degree in theology to tell people how much God loves them, and how they can come to Jesus and be born again. After all, those He left it to as He ascended were unlearned men. If God Himself baptizes you in the Holy Spirit, then you have a basic spiritual understanding of God's Word and be able to share what God is showing you. You will be equipped to share the saving gospel of Jesus Christ. Keep in mind that not everyone is called to teach however we are all called to spread the gospel of Christ. The Lord will equip you in a way that only He can do. The Lord is not looking for our ability. He is looking for our availability. If you seek God with all your heart and sincerely want more of him? Simply ask Him and He will be more than happy to give you more of Himself.

In my case, my parents came to the Lord in 1978. They received a prophecy that all their children would one day serve the Lord and we were all going to be used by God. It took many years for this to come to pass, but if anything is the Lord's plan, it will be fulfilled. God is never in a hurry He has time in His hands.

My mother came to me very excited one day to tell me she and my father had attended a church service and had gone up to the front for prayer. She said the minister came up to them and said, "The Lord says, that you have a son who is the most rebellious of all your children. He will come to me and serve me and I will use him for my glory." Wow! I remember thinking, Is that me? Is that how God sees me as a rebellious child? I don't want God to see me that way, because true rebellion takes place in the heart of a person and not just by their actions. I felt dirty and ashamed to find out that God saw me that way, but I always wondered why I never received a prophecy personally. Why did God tell others about me, but didn't tell me? Why can't I hear from God myself?

Well, guess what. I did hear from God. I heard His voice during my rebellious years. This is how it all started.

I will never forget the time I received my calling from God. It started when I was about 17 years old. I would stay out late hanging out with my friends as I mentioned in my book *A New Life Is Expecting You*. I was in a heavy metal band, and I would stay out late hours of the night, come home drunk, and wake up hung over most of the time. Well, this happened to me at least three different times.

The first time I heard the Lord's voice was in 1988. I was in my room fast asleep. I would cover my windows to make sure the sunlight wouldn't come in because I also had a night job, so it was common for me to sleep during the day. I heard my father calling my name. He would often work on the roof of our house. He would spread hot tar on our aluminum roof to seal holes and cracks. Whenever he called me, I would come to him, so he wouldn't have to be climbing up and down the ladder. Here is how it all started, I would be fast asleep, and I would hear his voice calling me, very softly "LEANDRO" with a short pause in between then again, I would hear "LE-AN-DRO" I would come running out of my room half asleep and say, "Yes dad, you called me?"

My father would look at me like I was crazy and say, "I didn't call you." I would say, "Dad, I heard your voice. I heard you call me," He said, "Go back and go to sleep. I never called you." When it happened again that same day a couple of hours later, this time he was in his room relaxing. I heard "Leandro" in a very soft but clear voice. It was almost as if it was a soft, clear whisper in my ear. I would come out again running, "Yes, dad. Did you call me?"

He looked at me with a curious stare, and said, "Son, I did not call you." Then he smiled and said, "Wait a minute! It is the Lord calling you. The next time you hear that voice say, 'Yes Lord I am here. Speak to me."

It reminded my father of the story of Samuel in the Bible, and how the same thing happened to him. Oh, my Lord, my jaw hit the floor! In awe, I felt as if I was walking back to my room in slow motion. I didn't know what to think. Was I hearing God's voice? Well, I had about two more hours to sleep before I had to get up for work, so I laid back down praying to God for the first time in a very long time. I started to doze off back when I heard it again. "Leandro." I said, "Yes Lord, I am here." My voice was trembling so that I could barely get the words out. Then I went into a deep sleep, I don't remember what happened next, but here is how it happened to Samuel in the bible.

1 Samuel 3:1-11 KJV

1) And the child Samuel ministered unto the Lord before Eli. And the word of the Lord was precious in those days; there was no open vision.

2) And it came to pass at that time when Eli was laid down in his place, and his eyes began to wax dim, that he could not see.

3) And ere the lamp of God went out in the temple of the Lord, where the ark of God was, and Samuel was laid down to sleep.

4) That the Lord called Samuel: and he answered, here am I.

5) And he ran unto Eli, and said, here am I; for thou called me. And he said, I called not; lie down again. And he went and lay down.

6) And the Lord called yet again, Samuel. And Samuel arose and went to Eli, and said, here am I; for thou didst call me. And he answered, I called not, my son; lie down again.

7) Now Samuel did not yet know the Lord, neither was the word of the Lord yet revealed unto him.

8) And the Lord called Samuel again the third time. And he arose and went to Eli, and said, Here am I; for thou didst call me. And Eli perceived that the Lord had called the child.

9) Therefore Eli said unto Samuel, Go, lie down: and it shall be, if he calls thee, that thou shalt say, Speak, Lord; for thy servant

> heareth. So, Samuel went and lay down in his place.
>
> 10) And the Lord came, and stood, and called as at other times, Samuel, Samuel. Then Samuel answered, Speak; for thy servant heareth.
>
> 11) And the Lord said to Samuel, Behold, I will do a thing in Israel, at which both the ears of everyone that heareth it shall tingle.

Isn't it amazing how God speaks to us? He is the same God yesterday, today, and forever. I get emotional every time I read or hear this story.

It took some time for me to understand that God wanted a deeper relationship with me. It took more than 25 years. Remember, God isn't in a hurry. He was reaching out to me, but I didn't understand what was missing in my life until God showed me that He was the one I longed for. Sometimes we get caught up in everyday life. Though we know there is a void in our lives that needs to be filled, we look elsewhere to fill the void. We search in all the wrong places to fill the void. We search for people, work, money, and relationships. We fail to remember that God wants more of us too. He wants more OF us, not more FROM us. He wants a closer relationship with us.

God loves to communicate with His people. He gives us chance after chance, but we continually mess things up. If you are longing for something, and you're not quite sure what it is, but know that something is missing in your life, it is likely God. You see, we are created with three parts: body, spirit, and soul. We are created in God's image. We too are a trinity. God is the Father, the Son, and the Holy Spirit the three in one.

King David would speak to his soul when he was depressed. He would ask his soul, "Why are you so downcast oh my soul?" He also commanded his soul to bless the Lord. He said, "Bless the Lord, O my soul." You can see it here in the Book of Psalms.

Psalm 42:1-11 KJV

1) As the hart panteth after the water brooks, so panteth my soul after thee, O God.

2) My soul thirsteth for God, for the living God: when shall I come and appear before God?

3) My tears have been my meat day and night, while they continually say unto me, where is thy God?

4) When I remember these things, I pour out my soul in me: for I had gone with the multitude, I went with them to the house of God, with the voice of joy and praise, with a multitude that kept holyday.

5) Why art thou cast down, O my soul? And why art thou disquieted in me? Hope thou in God: for I shall yet praise him for the help of his countenance.

6) My God, my soul is cast down within me: therefore, will I remember thee from the land of Jordan, and of the Hermonites, from the hill Mizar.

7) Deep calleth unto deep at the noise of thy waterspouts: all thy waves and thy billows are gone over me.

8) Yet the Lord will command his loving kindness in the daytime, and in the night his song shall be with me, and my prayer unto the God of my life.

9) I will say unto God my rock, why hast thou forgotten me? why go I mourning because of the oppression of the enemy?

10) As with a sword in my bones, mine enemies reproach me; while they say daily unto me, where is thy God?

11) Why art thou cast down, O my soul? and why art thou

> disquieted within me? Hope thou in God: for I shall yet praise him, who is the health of my countenance, and my God.

Here is another way to understand this. Suppose a person is in a coma in the hospital. They are breathing, but they're unconscious. Some who've experienced this, once they have recovered, report that while they were unconscious, they were looking down at their body the whole time. They say they could see and hear everyone who was in the room. That is because their body is on the bed, but their spirit is disconnected from the body seeing everything, and their soul is still in the body because the lungs still have breath.

This also proves that your brain, "your mind," is connected directly to your spirit and your soul is connected to your body. When a person is brain-dead, his spirit is still aware of his surroundings, and his soul is still in his body if he is breathing. He is still alive, even if being kept alive by machines. If he is still breathing, unconscious, yet spiritually awake, he can still trust Christ as his Savior.

A few years ago, my wife received a phone call from a family member asking if we would go and pray for her father, who was in hospice barely holding on to life. As my wife told me what was happening, we decided to pray first and ask God for direction and for His Holy Spirit to lead us. We arrived at the facility about thirty minutes later. We walked into his room and began to greet his family, who had gathered to say their goodbyes to him. I was led immediately by the Holy Spirit to acknowledge that he was still breathing and that he still had the life that I needed to speak directly to… his spirit. The family had told us that he had been unresponsive for days. I was led by the Holy Spirit to take his hand and introduce myself to him. I told him how I had heard from his loved ones that he was an awesome fisherman, and how I loved to fish as well, but wasn't very good at it. Out of respect for the family in this story, I will call him Hector.

I held Hector's hand and looked up to the corners of the room that we were in, and I said, "Hector, I know you are here with us. I also know you can see us, and that you can hear me. Hector, Jesus Christ sent me to let you know how much He loves you. He wants you to know that no matter how bad you were in your life, and no matter the mistakes you made, what are called sins. Jesus wants to forgive you today. Christ is the only one who can forgive you. That's because He is the one who died for our sins. Hector, this is your chance to make everything right between you and God. God sent me to you today so that you can be with Him in paradise forever. Hector, I need your Spirit to repeat this prayer after me. I need you to fight Hector, fight for your soul."

I held his forearm and said, "Death, I bind you, and you will have to wait in the name of Jesus Christ."

Then as I held his arm I said, "Hector, your family said that it's ok for you to go. They don't want you to suffer anymore. But Hector if you don't ask Jesus to forgive you and to come into your heart, you won't make heaven. Hector, I need for your spirit to fight and say this prayer. You can do it. With all your heart say, "Lord, I know I have sinned against you, forgive my sins. Jesus, I believe you are the Son of God who died for my sins and arose from the grave. Come into my heart and be my Savior and Lord. From this moment, I am saved. In Jesus' name, I pray. Amen."

While we were praying, he started to grunt, his eyelids were moving as if he was trying to open them. His fingers were twitching, and though his eyelids were closed, we could see his eyes moving as he grunted until we finished praying. He stopped moving and rested peacefully. Then I turned my attention to the family as I assured them that he had repeated that prayer and would now be in the kingdom of God. I also told them that if they ever wanted to see him again, they would have to come to Jesus Christ as Hector had.

I explained John 3:16 to them: "For God so loved the world, (that's us) that he gave his only begotten son, (Jesus Christ) That whosoever (that's us again) should not perish but have everlasting life." Then I led them in the prayer of salvation as well. Glory to God. My wife and I said our goodbyes to the family and about fifteen minutes later we received a call that Hector had passed on to be with the Lord. His daughter was so grateful that we had come, and that they had never seen or experienced anything like that before. I believe he was waiting for his family to tell him it was okay to let go; and then after receiving Christ, waited to see them join him. I'm certain he saw the spirit of death there to collect his soul. But what is exciting about all of this is that I also know he saw the angel of the Lord come into that room and death had to submit to the presence of the Lord. I have no doubt that Hector is now in the Lord's kingdom.

Here is why I believe that he is the kingdom of God. Because if his spirit calls out to God as he did, then he didn't have time to sin again before he died. The blood of Jesus Christ washes our sins away, Scripture says that He remembers our sins no more.

But if one were to accept Christ today and then tonight went out and got drunk and was in a fatal car accident while living outside of God's will and died in that sin, they wouldn't be in their right mind to call out to God at that moment. If one doesn't call on the name of the Lord, his soul can't be saved. Scripture says only those who call on the name of the Lord shall be saved. There is no salvation without repentance.

This next statement may cause an uproar in some because so many people have been taught "once saved always saved", which is not true. Some people choose to believe that no matter what, their loved one is in a better place. Friend, please stop fooling yourself. It may be easier to accept the lie, but the truth is the truth. Through Scripture, we are instructed to guard (protect) our salvation in Jesus Christ. I will now provide you with Scriptures to support what I have just said.

> John 3:16 - For God so loved the world that He gave His only begotten Son, that whoever believes in Him should not perish but have everlasting life.
>
> 1 Timothy 4:16 - Take heed unto thyself, and unto the doctrine; continue in them: for in doing this thou shalt both save thyself, and them that hear thee.
>
> James 1:15 - Then, after desire has conceived, it gives birth to sin; and sin, when it is full-grown, gives birth to death.
>
> Mathew 7:21 - "Not everyone who says to me, 'Lord, Lord,' will enter the kingdom of heaven, but only the one who does the will of my Father who is in heaven.

Don't you see how much the Lord loves us? Therefore, we should never make a judgment call if a sinner went to heaven or hell because we don't know if in their desperate moment before dying if they called out to God or not. That is not for us to know. Scripture also tells us that, "those that call on the name of the Lord shall be saved." We are to focus on our own spiritual condition. This requires us to turn from our sins and make every effort to sin no more. We don't earn salvation. We are saved by the grace of God and through our faith. We accept and live in that salvation. Don't you see? We must choose to live a righteous life. This requires a lifestyle change. But relax, this may take a little time for some depending on their situation. However, don't let that become your excuse. We still need to follow through with our decisions. Remember, "knowledge" is not power; "applied knowledge" is power! Apply God's Word to your life starting today.

WHAT IS SIN?

To get a full and clear understanding of sin, let's start here. One of the best ways that I can describe sin is a wall that separates us from God. Jesus Christ is the only one that can wash away our sins because He is the one who died on the cross in our place. Then what are sins? Sins are things that we have done wrong in our lifetime. It's in our blood. This is how we are born sinners. It's because of the blood that is running through our veins. We have the blood of our ancestors in our veins. Let's say that I had a great-grandparent who lived over 200 years ago who practiced witchcraft, and another who worshiped idols, and a third, who was an atheist and didn't believe in God. Now here I am, 200 years later having the blood of my ancestors in my veins. I am born a sinner, with a sinful nature.

Jesus Christ did not have this problem; His blood was pure. Mary, His mother, was a Virgin; Jesus was conceived of the Holy Spirit of God. Jesus remained sinless, and it is because His sinless blood was shed that we can have eternal life and be forgiven of our sins. Only the blood of Christ can wash away our sins and give us a new start. On the cross, Jesus Christ took our sins upon Himself and died in our place. Here is what is so amazing about our Lord.

When Satan and his demons thought they were killing Him, Jesus was taking upon Himself everything the devil had. He took it all and nailed it to the cross. Depression, hurt, and anxiety were nailed to His cross. You, my friend, have victory waiting for you through Jesus Christ. You don't have to deal with addictions, fear of rejection, or resentment anymore. You can be freed from all of that today. But the first thing you must do is be willing to meet Jesus with all your heart. Don't worry about being ready, just be willing. God will do the rest.

I once met a 90-year-old man in a Walmart bread aisle. He said, "Good morning, how are you doing?" I responded with, "I am great and better than I deserve by the grace of God." He smiled and said, "Do you think God has a plan for me? I am 90 years old. Ha, ha, ha!" I said, "Why wouldn't God have a plan for you? Moses was in his eighties; Daniel was in his eighties. What makes you think God doesn't have a plan for you?

God's first plan for all of us is to seek Him wholeheartedly. Yes, that means with all our hearts. Just like God told Jeremiah. Everybody likes to quote the feel-good verse in the bible.

> Jeremiah 29:11 - For I know the plans I have for you declares the Lord, plans to prosper you and not to harm you, plans to give you a hope and a future.

That's the feel-good verse that everyone loves because of the word "prosper." People see that word and think of money. They never bother to read the rest of that passage. Your real answer is in the next few verses that follow.

> 11:12 -Then you will call upon me and come and pray to me and I will listen to you.
>
> 11:13 - You will seek me and find me when you seek me with all your heart.
>
> 11:14 - I will be found by you, declares the Lord, and I will bring you back from captivity.

Don't you see? True power! The love of God for you, Just His word alone changes everything. There is power in the name of Jesus Christ. We are prisoners in our own minds through fear and anxiety. We deal with demonic oppression and demonization in our own mental and emotional states. We hold ourselves back from allowing God to save us and set us free. Before we came to Jesus the devil had us bound in sin, but when we gave our lives to Jesus, He set us free. But most Christians either don't understand their freedom in Christ or just don't know how to let go of the past. Look at it this way, I heard a brother in Christ many years ago explain it this way.

> Let's say you are in a prison cell. You are worshiping God from inside this prison cell, you are praising and thanking Him for setting you free. You're giving Him all the glory. But the problem is, you are still in your prison cell. Jesus says, "I died for more than this! Have you bothered to check your prison cell? The door is unlocked! It's open! The door to your prison cell is open. It's time to walk out and experience your freedom in Christ. That mental prison keeps us bound because we don't fully understand our salvation. We don't have a full understanding of what Jesus Christ did for us on the cross.

God has so much for you. He wants to heal you. God wants to set you free from all the curses that come from our sinful rebellion toward God. In God's eyes, no sin is great than another, a sin is a sin. Let God work in your heart starting today. Just remember this Jesus Christ loves you. He has a special plan for you. He wants you to come as you are, but He doesn't want you to stay that way. Be willing and He will do the work. God is calling you today will you answer His call?

Chapter 2

Called Into Action

I thought hard about writing this chapter. I did some heavy praying about it. There is too much fascination from the world with these types of subjects. People see this type of stuff in movies, but we deal with it in real life on a weekly, if not daily basis. People don't realize how real and dangerous it is. So, I decided to go ahead and write it to give God all the honor and glory. The devil is nothing more than a liar and a defeated foe. You must know that for the sake of respect and privacy I will change the names in this story.

A few years ago, I received a call from a young married couple asking for prayer. They had been experiencing problems in their marriage. I was invited to their home and asked if I would come and pray for them to see if Marcus, the husband, would open up to me a little. This way I would be able to help them figure out what direction the Lord would want us to take in prayer. It was a call to action from the Lord.

In my truck headed to their home, my nerves began to get the best of me. The devil was attacking my mind, telling me that I wasn't qualified to help Marcus. He was coming at me hard. I started to believe his lies. At one point I pulled over on the side of the road and considered just going home and telling them that something came up. I thought, "I'll go home and pretend that they are going to be okay." But I couldn't lie. I just couldn't do that to them. I felt a burst of inner strength come over me as I started to pray, rebuking that devil in the name of Jesus Christ.

After the prayer, I felt assurance and a sense of inner peace come over me as if I was being sent into a war zone.

As I pulled up to the house, I continued to pray and ask the Lord for wisdom. I rang the doorbell and was invited in. Marcus' wife Crystal answered the door and led me to the living room where he was. He said, "Hey brother, come on in," I shook his hand and asked to sit next to him because he said that he didn't want to talk too loudly. I thought that was a little strange, but okay, whatever.

Crystal left us alone, and I sat down next to Marcus. Through our conversation, I found out that he was keeping secrets from Crystal. I thought to myself, "Boom Red Flag!" That explains why he wanted the secrecy. That is rarely good for a marriage. Having secrets from your spouse is only going to cause problems on top of problems. He also confessed that he had a secret drinking problem, as well as a porn problem. He had been keeping that from his wife.

Marcus told me he and Crystal argued all the time and couldn't seem to get along. I wasn't surprised. As he talked, I was still asking the Lord for direction. Crystal politely knocked on the door offering us glasses of iced tea. She sat down next to me and asked if she could join us. Marcus said, "Yes, of course." Sitting with both, I silently asked God for wisdom and what I should say. Suddenly, I begin to share with them a bit of my life story and I mentioned to them that with God anything is possible. I began to show them how to turn their marriage in the right direction according to the Word of God.

I explained to them that God often uses areas where we have failed and struggled in to display His love, mercy, and His power. "For all we know," I told them, "God may use you two in a marriage counseling ministry after He has worked in your lives." This of course would take some time because God would first have to transform their hearts.

I explained how submitting to God was the first thing that needed to happen. I said, "If you keep secrets from each other, you must confess it to one another, so God can heal you individually and as a couple." I explained how God will not work through deception. I said, "Your healing is largely up to you. Do you believe that God can heal you? How open is your heart to receive His healing? It all comes down to you and your faith in God. For God to do His will in your life you have to submit wholeheartedly to Him. Remember, Jesus Christ said, "If you would only believe you would see the glory of God."

I did my best to always be there for Marcus and Crystal. Therefore, I was surprised when just a couple of days later Marcus called with one of the strangest phone calls I have ever received. The reason he called was to try and correct me, over a couple of Bible verses that I had posted on social media.

To tell you the truth I don't remember what the verses were. But he told me that God had visited him in a dream telling him that he was now a minister, and he was to reach out to some of the most well-known television preachers to join forces with them. He also mentioned that he would need to bring them into correction because they needed to be under his leadership. "Oh my gosh! You have got to be kidding me!" I said friend, "Who said this to you and how did you hear it?" I knew at that moment I was speaking to a demonic spirit of deception that had overtaken him.

Please keep in mind that we were speaking over the phone. So, I said, "In the name of Jesus Christ I bind you spirits of deception and delusion." As soon as I said those words, he began repeating, "la, la, la, la, over and over for a full minute. Then he started to repeat every word I would say to him. I recognized the spirit of mockery, and said, "I bind you spirit of mockery in the name of Jesus Christ."

For a few seconds, he got very quiet. Then he let out a loud yell and hung up the phone. I tried several times to call him back, but he wouldn't answer.

It was around eleven o'clock at night. I told my wife what had happened and knelt at my bedside and prayed for him.

About two days later while I was at work, I received a call on my cell phone. As it rang the Holy Spirit alerted me to pray before I answered. I immediately prayed covering myself with the blood of Jesus Christ. As soon as I said hello, a woman said, "Pastor Lenn, please come and help me. My husband won't stop screaming!" She sounded desperate, and I could hear her husband screaming, "Pastor Lenn, I need You! Please come help me! I need you!" Every time he would say something he would let out screams in between his words.

I said, "Call out to the Lord Jesus Christ! Ask Him to forgive you of your sins! You have sinned against God, it's His forgiveness that you need! He will help you right now."

His wife grabbed the phone hysterically, and said, "Can you please come or send someone!" She explained that she was afraid for her children and that the police would come because they lived in apartments and the neighbors might complain about his screaming.

Being at work, I couldn't just pick up and leave. So, I called a few pastors of some of the local churches, and evangelists that I respected. I called two of the biggest churches here in Corpus Christi, these were churches that are on radio and television, that host a lot of the big Christian concert events that come to town.

As someone answered the phone, I told them who I was and asked to speak with a pastor or prayer counselor. I began to explain the situation, and I asked if their deliverance team could go and minister to this tormented demon-possessed man. Here is what I got from both churches, "Ha-ha we don't do that here, all they need is to come to Jesus, there is no need for all that deliverance stuff."

I said, "What? Are you kidding me? You are a pastor, and you don't believe in this? You must be joking! If you don't believe in deliverance through Jesus Christ, then what in the world do you preach and teach? The Bible tells us that this was the ministry of Jesus Christ."

> Jesus Christ himself said in Luke 4:18 - "The Spirit of the Lord is on me, because he has anointed me to proclaim good news to the poor. He has sent me to proclaim freedom for the prisoners and recovery of sight for the blind, to set the oppressed free."

Jesus was saying the Father had anointed Him to bring good news "to the poor", meaning those who were lost and bound in sin. He came to free spiritual prisoners, those bound by Satan, to heal blind eyes, and free those oppressed in spiritual darkness. He was referring to spiritual strongholds that the devil or demons could have on a person or family that may struggle, mentally, spiritually, physically, and emotionally. This includes fear, depression, anxiety, addiction, sickness, and more. The devil keeps people oppressed and imprisoned. Jesus came to set us free from the devil's grip.

He also said He came to "restore sight to the blind". He is referring to physical blindness as well as spiritual blindness. Many people don't believe in Jesus Christ or are confused about who God is.

Here is a quick example: *Allah* is the Arabic word for god. Some then assume that our God is *Allah.* But we serve the one true living God, Creator of all things, and Father of our Lord Jesus Christ. He has many names, but *Allah* is NOT one of them. *Allah* is the moon god worshipped by Muslims. That is an example of those who are confused about who God is.

How could these Bible teachers say that they don't believe in deliverance through Christ when He said we who follow Him will do what He did, in His name? The devil and every demonic spirit will submit at the mention of His name. His name is our authority. He told us this in Luke 14:12, *"Truly I say to you that whoever believes in me will also do the works that I do, and he will do even greater things because I am going to the father."*

I was beside myself; how could this be? So, I phoned the couple and suggested they come to church the following Sunday and that after the morning service, we would minister to them both. Why would I want to sit around and wait for someone else to do what God has called me to do? I called the senior pastors of my church, along with a couple of faithful spirit-filled church members, and we each got in agreement with the Lord and fasted the rest of the week. As we prayed, we asked for direction, for the Holy Spirit's anointing to fill us, and for the Lord to do the work through us for His glory and honor.

SHUT UP DEVIL

Understand. What you are about to read is real. When I say that God wants to take us to a new level, this is what I'm talking about.

Sunday, as instructed, they arrived for their deliverance session with our team. During the week we had been fasting and binding the devil just as Jesus told us to do in Matthew 12:29 and Mark 3:27. So, by the time the couple arrived at the church we had everything in place, and the Holy Spirit was ready to set them both free. In the background we had two people singing worship and praises to the Lord. One person on the team took the lead to administer the deliverance session.

In preparation we had the couple write down a week in advance everything they have ever felt and their current symptoms. This helps a great deal for the day of the deliverance. We have been told that people even start to feel strange a day or two before they arrive. They may start crying uncontrollably for no reason whatsoever. This usually happens around the time they are counseled to pray and write down every unnatural behavior and feelings that they have experienced.

Usually, after one lists "depression", is when this starts to happen because that spirit is fully aware that it is about to be cast out, and it will start to manifest itself. Here are a few others that have done the same thing when they know that they are about to be confronted. Rebellion, hurt, rejection, fear of rejection, anger, anxiety, suicidal thoughts, homosexuality, bitterness, unforgiveness, and others.

In this case, their lists were different. We ministered to one person at a time. The very first step is always to lead them to salvation because people have different opinions and understanding of what salvation through Jesus Christ is. We then began by reading scriptures about when Jesus would set people free and about the Lord's promises to His people. We then read scriptures about the authority that has been given to us through Christ. You can read this in Luke 10:19 "Behold, I have given you authority to trample on snakes and scorpions and over all the power of the enemy, and nothing by any means will harm you."

I then said the words, "In the name of Jesus Christ, I bind you unclean, foul, demonic Spirits along with all of your companions, we are covered in the blood of Jesus Christ, the Messiah and no weapon formed against us will prosper." As soon as I finished saying the words "in the name of Jesus," Marcus crossed his legs and his hands. Immediately his hands shot back behind his body, and he started screaming as if he was tied up and in agony. We had him renounce every evil spirit by telling each spirit that it was no longer welcomed inside him because he has been bought with the blood of Jesus. As Marcus was renouncing each demonic spirit, it would resist us, each one would manifest differently. I would say something, and Marcus would repeat whatever I said with a glazed look in his eyes,

I knew this was a spirit of "mockery". Then mockery would be cast out. Then the next one would show up and his nose would be up high in the air and his arms would cross. That was the spirit of "pride". Then it would be cast out. The next one would show up and I would say,

"Come out in the name of Jesus." Each would speak in a different voice. But one kept saying, "No, no, no." The Holy Spirit showed me it was "Rebellion". This continued for about forty-five minutes to an hour. Marcus had a three-page list that we went through. But most importantly the Holy Spirit guides us through deliverance ministry. One demon manifested itself, causing Marcus to foam at the corners of his mouth and drool. The look in his eyes would change.

Marcus' eyes would be dilated for one spirit, then suddenly change with the next demon. And always with a lot of screaming. The demons were trying to stall us. We insisted that Marcus keep his eyes open because closing their eyes is another way demons will stall. We would not engage in a conversation with the demons because that is another way they stall. After about an hour Marcus became peaceful and was slain in the Spirit. We continued worshipping God with songs of praise and worship.

When Marcus came to his senses a short while later, he remembered everything but said that he couldn't control anything. He said that he was fully aware of what was happening. He slowly started to get the color back on his face and his smile came back as he gave God the glory. Friends, he was set free because he was willing to let God change him. Jesus tells us that if only believe, we will see the glory of God. Both Marcus and Crystal have been set free since that day. All glory to our King of Kings and Lord of Lords, Jesus Christ.

No matter what you are facing, friend if you only believe you will also see the glory of God in your life. I have experienced it myself. I have seen it with my own eyes since I was ten years old. The spirit world is quite real. Many times, the spirits that put up a fight and do not want to come out of a person are usually deeply rooted in their souls. I realize that this may sound like a fantasy world to some people, but the truth is the truth and when it comes to the truth, I don't care about anyone's opinions unless they too have seen it with their own eyes.

Because unless you have faced it up close and in person, the only thing you can do is imagine and speculate what you think it's like. But it's rarely the same. Some demons come out without a fight, and some put up a fight. But we never look for a spiritual fight. But in the name of Jesus Christ, we are always ready for one and it is the Holy Spirit who does everything.

If we are filled with the Holy Spirit those evil, unclean spirits will recognize Him. He is who they back down from. They do not back down from us. The fear the Holy Spirit. He is God. Therefore, we must be real before God, lest our spiritual life is compromised. There is a story of this in the Bible that supports what I am telling you.

<u>Matthew 17:14-21 KJV</u>

Jesus Heals a Demon-Possessed Boy

14) And when they were come to the multitude, there came to him a certain man, kneeling to him, and saying,

15) Lord, have mercy on my son: for he is lunatic, and sore vexed: for ofttimes he falleth into the fire, and oft into the water.

16) And I brought him to thy disciples, and they could not cure him.

17) Then Jesus answered and said, O faithless and perverse generation, how long shall I be with you? How long shall I suffer you? Bring him hither to me.

18) And Jesus rebuked the devil; and he departed out of him: and the child was cured from that very hour.

19) Then came the disciples to Jesus apart, and said, why could not we cast him out?

20) And Jesus said unto them, Because of your unbelief: for verily I say unto you, if ye have faith as a grain of mustard seed, ye shall

> say unto this mountain, remove hence to yonder place; and it shall remove; and nothing shall be impossible unto you.
>
> 21) Howbeit this kind goeth not out but by prayer and fasting

I hope you caught that! We see a few major life-changing spiritual facts here. We see that epilepsy (the seizures) is an evil spirit in verse eighteen. Then we see that the disciples were unable to cast it out, because of their unbelief. How can anyone expect to see a miracle if they don't believe? Remember Jesus said if we would only believe, we would see the glory of God. Our faith is a major key to unlocking God's glory in our lives.

In verse twenty-one, we see that this kind of evil spirit only comes out with spiritual preparation, like prayer and fasting. Prayer and fasting are putting ourselves aside so that we can be led by the Holy Spirit. If we are not spiritually prepared, like the disciples in this story, God won't be able to use us. So, get ready. People all around us need a miracle from God. Fast, pray and seek more of God so He can use you for His Glory. He has greater purposes waiting for you.

If you find yourself in need and if any part of this story is hitting "too close to home" then please find a Holy Spirit-filled Church that teaches the full gospel of Jesus Christ. Do your part to make every effort to get close to the Lord by reading His word, praying, and fasting according to Scripture.

Start by reading the books of Matthew, Mark, Luke, and John. The reason I recommend these books is that they are where you will find Jesus healing people. In simple terms, we need one of two types of healing. We either need demons cast out of us like many people in the Bible did, or we need God's healing touch. The lady who touched the Lord's garment and was healed had made her way to him and was healed according to her faith. Her mind was set on having an encounter with the Lord.

Also, remember the blind man in John 9 who needed the Lord's healing touch. Don't fool yourself by thinking if you are dealing with something severe like anxiety or hopelessness you just need prayer and God's healing touch. If you have a demon, then you most likely have more than one. One "opens the door" to let the next one in, then they work together to destroy a person's life.

Please reach out to a church near you and have a one-on-one conversation with the pastor. We would be happy to serve you. Please feel free to contact our ministry and let us know how. It all starts with you taking the first step. You are called into action. Will you answer the Lord's call? Friend, our Lord Jesus Christ loves you and is waiting to hear from you. It is a simple process; don't complicate things. Just open your mouth and let your heart do the talking.

LEANDRO OLIVAREZ

Chapter 3

Destination Heaven

What I am about to share with you is all about living, it is something that happened and through the grace of God, I had the pleasure of being involved in this life-changing moment. Throughout this book, you have been reading about life and living and planting seeds to make a difference in someone else's life. Remember when it involves the Lord God almighty, there are no limits to what He can do. This was for me a life-changing moment that I will never forget.

I was driving through a small town one day when I decided to exit the freeway and go to another town nearby. I wanted to look at some real estate I was interested in. As I took the exit, I immediately regretted doing so thinking, there is nothing I want in that town. So, I decided to get back on the highway as soon as I could.

As I approached a stop sign, I quickly realized that a train had come to a complete stop and was blocking the road. There was no doubt I had taken a wrong turn. This would take too much time. Because of the train, all the traffic was forced to take the turnaround and circle back to get back on the freeway.

As I entered the turnaround, my phone began to ring, and as soon as it did, I looked and saw my brother-in-law was calling. I answered the call, "Hello". My brother-in-law, Rick, on the other end said, "Hey Lenn, I need for you to go to Corpus Christi to pick up an order for me." As soon as he said those words, I approached a yield sign, and that very moment I heard a loud screech, followed by a loud BOOM!

I told Rick, "Awe man! I've got to go, there is a car wreck in front of me, and I must go render aid. It's against the law if I don't!" He replied,

"Stay on the phone with me!" There was one car in front of me. Two young girls climbed out of their car and ran with me to one of the wrecked vehicles. We arrived at the vehicle at the same time.

Not seeing anyone in the car, I asked the two girls if they could see anyone. Then I stuck my head in the shattered car window and saw an elderly woman's hand raised. I asked the girls to call 911. But they looked at me and took off running back to their car. I didn't wait. I had my phone in my hand and I could hear Rick when I said that we needed to call 911, he said, "Okay, call me back!"

As I made the 911 call, I began talking to the lady in the front seat. I said, "Ma'am can you hear me?" She reached out to me and said, "I can't breathe." So, I reached back, grabbed her hand, and said, "Ma'am, I'm going to slowly pull you toward me to sit you up so you can breathe. We are going to go very slowly. Just make a noise if it hurts and I will stop." She said softly, "Okay."

All I could do was pray for her. I said, "Ma'am may I pray for you? Will you pray with me?" She said she would. "May I hold your hand?" I asked. She took my hand. She was trembling, had a busted lip, and a little blood on her arm. I told her to relax, close her eyes, and repeat after me. The only thing that came to my mind were the words, "Help me, Lord Jesus. Help me, Lord Jesus Christ." She was repeating every word that I was saying in the prayer.

I gently cleaned the shattered glass from her car window off her face and picked the glass out of her hair. Then I asked. "Do you hurt anywhere?" She said, "Oh yes, I hurt all over. My chest hurts." I said, "Try to relax, an ambulance is on the way." I felt as if the sound of the wind and the sound of the passing traffic had shut off. For a moment, I couldn't hear anything, All I could hear was my own heart pounding in my chest. The silence was so loud. I was asking the Lord what I should do. "Lord, what do I say?" All that kept coming to my mind was having her say, "Help me, Lord Jesus Christ." I asked her name. She told me, and from that moment, I never stopped calling her by her name.

A truck had hit her car, then it careened off the road and over the railroad tracks. A man who stopped to help went to check on the driver of the truck, and then came to the lady's car. I moved over so he could lean through the window to turn off the ignition.

I had to let go of her hand for a few seconds to let the man pass in front of me. When I let go of her hand, she looked at me as if to say, "Please, don't leave me." I told her, "I am not going to leave you. I am right here. Continue to call on the Lord." Every time I would tell her to call upon the Lord, she would do it without hesitation. She reached out to me and said, "Hold my hand." I reached under the guy's arm and grabbed her hand.

When he moved out of the way I asked if she had any children I should call. She said, "Yes, my daughter, lives close by." "Do you have a cell phone, or her phone number so I can call her?" She tried to move and said, "I don't know where it could be." I said, "Never mind, don't worry about it. When you get to the hospital, they will notify your family." I looked up and realized that we were on a busy street.

Cars were still zooming by, and people were in a panic, running to check on the other vehicle. Several asked if we had called 911.

I won't share her name, out of respect for her and her family. However, she changed my life forever. The look in her eyes was a look of both fear and peace if that makes any sense. She asked me to please open the door. I told her it would be best if we didn't, in case she had internal injuries, or was hurt below her waist. She was frustrated and wanted to move around. I knew she was in shock, and told her, "Lean your head back, and I'll clean you up a little more."

I continued to pray with her calling out to the Lord Jesus. The police arrived and walked up to the scene. I told the officer her name, and that she was in pain all over her body, that her chest was hurting, and that she was having trouble breathing. The officer asked if I had called 911. I said, "Yes, I called seconds after impact."

He said, "Ma'am, do you have your driver's license?" I said, "Sir, she is an elderly woman, and she is hurt! She is having trouble breathing!" He leaned in and said, "Ma'am the ambulance is on its way, don't worry I'll get your ID from you later." Then he told me he was going to check on the other driver.

She was in such pain; all I could think to do was keep telling her to call out to the Lord Jesus. She would. "Help me, Lord Jesus Christ," she would say. It was crucial that she did. Here is why. Scripture says, in Romans 10:13: "For whosoever shall call upon the name of the Lord shall be saved."

I honestly believe she cried out to the Lord with all her heart. I wanted to make sure I did not disappoint the Lord because by then, I understood the reason for my "wrong turn." I told her, "I will not leave your side until the ambulance arrives."

For what seemed like hours, I held her hand, because I wanted to keep her calm. But I wondered where in the world the ambulance was. She leaned her head over toward me and said in a gentle voice, "Please open the door." Again, I said I couldn't lest she have further injuries. I reminded her that the ambulance is almost there.

I could not stop thinking of my mother. I would want someone to be with my mother if the tables were turned. I kept thinking about how I wished I could notify her family. I told her to keep calling out to God on her way to the hospital. I said, "The Lord is with you, don't be afraid." I prayed for the Lord to give her peace and for the Holy Spirit to embrace and comfort her.

Then, as if someone turned up the volume, I heard sirens, people's voices, and even heard the wind blowing. "The ambulance is here," I told her, calling her by name. "They will take care of you from here, you will see your family soon. I am going to leave you now, but the Lord is with you. Keep calling out to Jesus Christ."

I turned to tell the paramedic her name and where she told me she was hurting, then walked back to my car. As I sat down, I thanked the Lord for sending me to her side and took a picture of her car in hopes of notifying her family on social media. Along with the photo, I posted, "I just witnessed this horrible accident here in Gregory, Texas. I stayed with the woman involved, praying with her until the ambulance arrived. Her name is, (her name) and she said that she has a daughter named (daughters name) who lives here." Then to my surprise, a lady who I know, who with her family visits our church from time to time responded to my post saying the injured lady was her grandmother!

This was horrible, I knew this family. About an hour later, my sister called to tell me that someone had commented on my post that the woman from the accident had passed away. I said, "There is no way. She was alert and spoke with me the whole time. I never left her side. She wanted me to open the door and help her out of the car. I held her hand. There must be some mistake." My sister said, "You never know, Lenn. She certainly could have had internal injuries. You should call the family to check on her." I was still at work and almost as soon as I hung up the phone, the daughter of the woman who passed away said the words I did not want to hear. She said, "Pastor we lost my mom."

Oh, my Lord, I could not believe what I was hearing. My heart sank, the world was spinning, and I had to compose myself. So, I went to the hospital to pray with the family, offer my support, and share with them my time with their precious mother. I didn't have words to express my feelings. Although I thought that I had taken the wrong turn, it turned out to be the turn the Lord wanted me to take.

We never know when we are going to be with someone in their final moments. As I left the family and walked through the hospital parking lot, and sat in my car, I cried and thanked the Lord for putting me in her path. "Lord, I just sent someone to your Kingdom. Be with her family. Give them peace in their hearts." Though I was heartbroken, I felt complete peace at the same time. This is true POWER!

Each of us who are in Christ has the Holy Spirit along with His fire in us. We have authority in the spirit realm to change circumstances in the name of Jesus Christ. But the true expression of power is when the devil is trying to destroy someone and take them to hell, and we step in, cancel the devil's plans, and redirect them to heaven where one day we will see them again. That is not a sense of personal accomplishment. It's simply God's love, mercy, and power on display. That is the power in you through Christ.

If we keep our minds on the Lord and communicate with him continually, we will be surprised where the Lord will send us, and how he will use us. We need to be ready to plant the life-giving seeds of the gospel. "But she died," one might say. No, she is very much alive now. She called out to the Lord in her final moments. The gospel seeds he had given me to plant, quickly took root, and sprang to eternal life! Her Spirit life was just beginning. Today she is in heaven, and able to approach the Lord's throne.

Please apply the following statements to your life. She and I were going in the same direction on two different paths. Is the path you are on right now taking you in the wrong direction? If so, what if in your final moments there is no one there to bring you to Jesus? What then?

Come to Jesus today while you have time. Don't wait another minute. Tomorrow is not guaranteed. After our final breath here, there are only two places we can go. One is the heavenly Kingdom of God; the other is the place of torment in outer darkness that is prepared for Satan and his demons. This is the truth. A thousand years from today our souls will live on, the question is where?

The decision you make today determines your eternal destination. God leaves that decision with you. If he controlled us, then why would it be so important for us to choose him? He won't override your free will.

Today is the day of salvation, if you are reading this it's not too late to surrender to Jesus Christ. Come on over, He is waiting for you. Don't let circumstances choose for you.

LEANDRO OLIVAREZ

Chapter 4

Inner Prison

One Sunday while I was in church playing the drums during the praise and worship, I realized that I wanted to sing along to one of the songs. I believe we were singing the song, *How Great Is Our God*. Suddenly, I realized that I could not open my mouth. I felt tired and couldn't get the strength to do something as simple as open my mouth. I knew instantly what was happening. The devil was trying to keep me from worshiping God in the Spirit. In case you don't know, I am the drummer for the praise and worship team as well as the Associate Pastor of the church.

As soon as the music is over, I always make my way to the pulpit to deliver the message for the service. So, I knew I was under a spiritual attack that morning.

I stepped up to the pulpit and mentioned to the congregation what was happening to me during the worship. As soon as I filled everyone in on what had taken place they reached out their hands and we began to bind every unclean, evil, and foul spirit in the name of Jesus Christ.

We prayed,

> "Heavenly Father your Word says that" whatever we bind on earth will be bound in heaven, and whatever we loose on earth will be loosed in heaven. In the mighty name of Jesus, the Christ, our messiah, your Son, our Savior we plead the blood of Jesus over every man, woman, and child here today. We bind the unwelcomed evil and unclean spirits of distraction, heaviness, worry, hurt, fear, rejection, and control

along with all their companions. Devils, you are not welcome here, and in the name of Jesus, we take authority over you and command you to leave right now and take all your companions with you, NOW! We command you in the name of Jesus Christ to go now!"

As soon as we finished the prayer the whole church went right into worship. It was a beautiful thing to see the prayer warriors step into action.

You should have been there. Everyone in the church was praying in the spirit. It was a beautiful, soft, and warm feeling as if every care in the world had been lifted from each of us. One could hear some people praying and others worshiping in tongues, while others sang softly in the background. Scripture tells us to submit to God, resist the devil and he will flee.

Notice the first step in that order? First, we are to submit to God. This isn't always an easy thing to do. But here is how I have learned to submit to God. I am going to share some very "private heartbeats" with you right now.

When my spirit feels weak, and it feels like my burdens and fears outweigh my blessings, I remind myself that this is not true.

The first step I take is to remember the difference between my "carnal mind" and my "spiritual mind." The carnal mind is when we act or think like our "old self". Most Christians, it seems, have not yet learned to distinguish between the two. Being able to distinguish between them gives us a clearer understanding of where we are, and were we need to be in our spiritual walk with the Lord.

One of the biggest problems in the Church today is too many people are giving God their carnal worship. They arrive at church, do their routine, then return home as they were. God has so much more than that for us. He wants to have a deep spiritual encounter with us so we can be set free from our inner prison. Here is an example of what I'm referring to as "carnal worship."

Let's say that one is sitting in church with their spouse and child. They are talking with their spouse and scolding their child at the same time the praise team is leading a worship song. The person behind you is singing, with their hands raised, and peaceful tears rolling down their cheeks.

COLOSSIANS 3:1-17

Not Carnality but Christ

1) If then you were raised with Christ, seek those things which are above, where Christ is, sitting at the right hand of God.

2) Set your mind on things above, not on things on the earth.

3) For you died, and your life is hidden with Christ in God.

4) When Christ who is our life appears, then you also will appear with Him in glory.

5) Therefore put to death your members which are on the earth: fornication, uncleanness, passion, evil desire, and covetousness, which is idolatry.

6) Because of these things the wrath of God is coming upon the sons of disobedience,

7) In which you yourselves once walked when you lived in them.

8) But now you yourselves are to put off all these: anger, wrath, malice, blasphemy, filthy language out of your mouth.

9) Do not lie to one another, since you have put off the old man with his deeds,

10) And have put on the new man who is renewed in knowledge according to the image of Him who created him,

11) Where there is neither Greek nor Jew, circumcised nor uncircumcised, barbarian, Scythian, slave nor free, but Christ is all and in all.

The Character of the New Man

12) Therefore, as the elect of God, holy and beloved, put on tender mercies, kindness, humility, meekness, longsuffering;

13) Bearing with one another, and forgiving one another, if anyone has a complaint against another; even as Christ forgave you, so you also must do.

14) But above all these things put on love, which is the bond of perfection.

15) And let the peace of God rule in your hearts, to which also you were called in one body: and be thankful.

16) Let the word of Christ dwell in you richly in all wisdom, teaching and admonishing one another in psalms and hymns and spiritual songs, singing with grace in your hearts to the Lord.

17) And whatever you do in word or deed, do all in the name of the Lord Jesus, giving thanks to God the Father through Him.

We the Lord's people must put on Christ, in all things. It can be hard to worship and focus on the Lord when surrounded by carnal Christians. We are singing along trying to get into the spirit, then it begins. The people around you start getting after their children saying, "Stop that! Sit still!"

They sing some more, then say to their spouse, "No honey. I don't have the keys to the car."

> After singing some more, they turn back to their children, "Turn around and pay attention!"
> Singing some more, then to their spouse, "Psstt! Did you see who just walked in?"
> Then to feel like they are fitting in, they shout "Glory to God!"
> Then they wave their "spirit fingers."

That is an example of carnal worship. God is not interested one bit in our carnal worship. So, there you have it, learn to recognize when and if you are operating in the carnal mind. Other names for this are our "sin nature" or "our flesh". Once you can identify and recognize the difference, examine yourself. Be better aware of your true spiritual condition you will be able to take the proper steps in the right direction to correct the problem by disconnecting your mind from everything and everyone around you and focusing completely on Christ.

Here is how I started doing this. I would get a vision of Jesus Christ in my mind of Him on the cross, and the physical condition He was in. I can only imagine the brutality that my Savior took upon Himself for all of humanity. I know it was the worst mankind has ever seen because we still talk about it today over 2000 years later. This is a good place to start.

I imagine I'm looking at him, and with my eyes shut, I focus on him as if I am standing at the foot of His cross, next to His mother and brother. While on my knees, I thank Him for taking my place and dying for me, so I can be forgiven of everything I have ever done wrong. That way I can be healed from every kind of sickness and disease, so I can be with him in heaven. Jesus not only took our place at the cross, but he gave us His place in heaven.

Now I do my best to get another picture in my heart and mind. I direct my vision to Jehovah God my Father. I recall how He had to turn His face from Christ the moment when Jesus became sin on the cross. God is too holy to be in the presence of sin. He never left Jesus, but He knew this had to be done for us. These were the Father's orders.

> John 3:16 - For God so loved the world (That's us) that he gave His only begotten Son (Jesus) that whosoever (that's us) believes in him (Jesus) will not perish (in hell) but have everlasting Life. (In heaven)

Next, I will begin by thanking God the Father, for sending His son Jesus Christ. I tell Him who He is to me. I begin with His name as I draw my mental, emotional, physical, and spiritual focus completely to Him. Sometimes I kneel quietly for a few minutes and don't utter a word until my mind is completely only on Him. That means, I get to the point where I don't hear the kids calling me, or the TV in the next room. My mind is only wrapped around God.

At this time, I began to speak His name in righteous submission, and I may worship Him in song. I know that I am speaking to the Creator of all things.

> "Heavenly Father you are *EL Shaddai, EL Elohim*. Lord, you are *Adonai, Yahweh, Jehovah Nissi, Jehovah Rapha*.
>
> Lord you are *Majesty*, you are *Holy*.
> Lord, you are *the Great I AM*, the *Highest God, Lord God Almighty, Jehovah Jireh*, the *Lord my Provider*, the *Alpha*, and *Omega*.
> Lord you are the *Beginning* and the *End*, you are the *Lord my Banner*, you are *Elohim*.
> You are my Healer.
> Lord, you are the one true *Living God*.
> You are the *Everlasting God*, my *Peace*.

> Without you Father, I can do nothing!
> You are *King of Kings* and *Lord of Lords*.
> You are *Abba Father*; you are my *Refuge*.
> Heavenly Father I incline your ear to you as I worship your Holy Name.

I will quietly sing to Him as I envision myself on my knees or even on my face at the foot of His throne. I'll sing the worship chorus *Alleluia* several times, then *Oh How I Love Jesus* several times. Then I'll sing *How Great Is Our God.* As my mind is completely focused on Him, I offer Him all that I have as well as all that I am. This includes my job, my vehicles, my home, my ministry, my family, my talents, my speech, my mind, body, spirit, and soul. This is a major step in a meaningful encounter with the Holy Spirit.

Try it. Don't hold back anymore. It is your time to step into the position that God Almighty has created for you. Come on it's your turn to give of yourself to Him. You are the special gift that God wants. No more holding back. Let today be the day you experience the Holy Spirit's presence.

Often, our past hurts and fears, many of which lie hidden inside us, become like a mental prison, keeping us in bondage. Many times, our emotions get the best of us to the point that the devil paralyzes us with fear, keeping us from moving forward with Jesus Christ. Keep in mind if you are a born-again child of God, you possess the authority through Jesus Christ to break those chains of depression, rejection, fear, and every unclean spirit that comes against you.

> Luke 10:19 Behold, I give unto you power to tread on serpents and scorpions, and over all the power of the enemy: and nothing shall by any means hurt you.

One of the main reasons people around the world give up on life and commit suicide is because they have lost hope. They are hopeless. We weren't created to simply exist and to try to figure out life ourselves. God created us for His purpose to live a life of spiritual freedom through Him. We search the world for something that it can't offer. Only Christ, because of what He did for us on the cross, can offer us redemption, the forgiveness of our sins, and guide us through this life with His Holy Spirit. We must remember that Jesus Christ IS OUR HOPE!

Only Jesus shed His blood for us. If you find yourself wanting to give up on life the very first thing you need to do is call out to Him and return to Him with all your heart. He alone is your true hope. So, if you don't have hope, then invite Jesus into your heart. At this point, you must make the effort as soon as possible to come back to Him. It is through Him that we have eternal life.

<u>Jeremiah 29:11-14</u>

> 11) For I know the plans that I have for you,' declares the LORD, 'plans for welfare and not for calamity to give you a future and a hope.
>
> 12) Then you will call upon Me and come and pray to Me, and I will listen to you.
>
> 13) You will seek Me and find Me when you search for Me with all your heart.
>
> 14) I will be found by you,' declares the LORD, 'and I will restore your fortunes and will gather you from all the nations and from all the places where I have driven you,' declares the LORD, 'and I will bring you back to the place from where I sent you into exile.'

The key is to seek Him with all your heart and cry out to Him because He tells us that He will respond. He will take us out of the land of captivity, that mental prison that we have built thinking it will protect us from being hurt. The truth is, the devil uses that wall to keep us bound using seclusion, hurt, unforgiveness, and distrust. It is the devil's grip on our mind, body, spirit, and soul. The devil is working round the clock to keep us from God.

I mentioned this in my first book, *A New Life Is Expecting You,* the reason the devil hates you so much is that God loves you so much. Think about it, if someone were to hurt your family, the best way to get back at that person is not to attack them, but to hurt their family. We hurt more deeply when our loved ones are hurt. Therefore, the devil attacks us because he knows that if he can get us away from God and destroys our faith and wipes us out and we die without Christ then he knows he hurts God. Because God loves us so much that he sent his son Jesus to die for us so that we can be with him in paradise forever.

> John 3:16 - For God so loved the world, that he gave his only begotten Son, that whosoever believeth in him should not perish, but have everlasting life.
>
> Luke 4:18 - The Spirit of the Lord is upon me, because he hath anointed me to preach the gospel to the poor; he hath sent me to heal the brokenhearted, to preach deliverance to the captives, and recovering of sight to the blind, to set at liberty them that are bruised,

I love that verse because it speaks about the recovery of sight for the blind. Jesus is mainly speaking of spiritual blindness. Many people are so spiritually blind they can't see the truth is Jesus Christ. This is exactly where your turning point is. When you come to Jesus, He will remove the blinders as well as every mind-binding stronghold in your life. This is at the cross of Calvary where you will be set free from all your spiritual baggage. The cross of Jesus is where the blood flowed, and the earth quaked because our Savior lives! He lives so that we can have eternal life free of bondage and demonic oppression. This is the truth you are looking for. *Jesus said He is the truth.*

> John 14:6 - I am the way, the truth, and the life, No one comes to the father but by me.

I encourage you to seek Jesus Christ with all your heart today. Remember, there is no sin greater than Jesus. There is no trial that you will ever face that is bigger than our God. Scripture tells us in Romans 8:37 that through Christ we are more than conquerors! It does not say we are conquerors through Christ. It says we are MORE than conquerors.

This puts us above every circumstance that we will ever face. When we receive Christ, our past sins no longer matter. He forgives, cleanses, and promises never to remember them again. Once we come to Christ with all our hearts, the devil can no longer hold those past sins against us.

> Today is your day to strip the devil of his spiritual legal rights over you and your family. Come to Jesus as you are right now, willing to change and to be changed. Understand that we all come as sinners because we were all born sinners. Sadly, some people have the mentality, "I am a good person. God loves me exactly the way I am. If He wants me to change then when He's ready, He'll change me. But until then I am who I am." Scripture says, "There is none good, no not one.... For all have sinned and come short of the glory of God." (Romans 3:10, 23)

Friend, Jesus wants you to come to Him the way you are, but He doesn't intend for you to remain in your sin. That is why He washes away our sins with His blood. If we think we are fine the way, we are then what would we need God for in the first place? We must turn from our sins and do our part to sin no more. That is why we are to guard our salvation and repent to our Lord daily. Sinners will not be allowed into the kingdom of heaven in a sinful nature condition, however, Sinners who've repented of their sins will be permitted to enter. This simple fact is the reason that God sent his son Jesus Christ to die for our sins is so we may have eternal life.

God is ready to do a mighty work in you, but you must be willing to let Him. He is already at work behind the scenes in your life. Do you remember the words of Jesus Christ? "If you will only believe you would see the Glory of God!" It's time for you to break free from that mental, spiritual, emotional, physical, and financial land of captivity. Your children and your great-grandchildren will benefit from your faith, somebody in your bloodline must have the faith in the Lord to step out in faith and believe in the blood of Jesus to break the curses in your bloodline.

You may not believe what I am saying and that's fine. But if this is you, examine your situation. Are you healthy? Are all your family members healthy? Do you struggle with your finances? Do you struggle with your family members? Be honest with yourself. Does any of this describe any part of your situation? Fight for yourself and fight for the spiritual freedom of your family. If there is a real problem, then you must recognize there is a problem. If you truly do not see a problem when everyone around you is telling you that there is one, then chances are *you* are the problem. You must humble yourself and be honest for your own sake and the sake of your loved ones. This is the first step to your freedom, as well as the freedom of the people you love. So, with that in mind, if you believe in the mighty powerful name of Jesus Christ, now I declare your spiritual freedom and command every wall of sin and mental and emotional chaos to come down. Be free in the name of Jesus Christ, I pray. Amen.

Chapter 5

Overcoming Depression

After careful consideration and extensive review of this topic of depression, we will look at the spiritual side of depression. Here is the dictionary definition of depression.

de·pres·sion:

NOUN- feelings of severe despondency and dejection.

1. "self-doubt creeps in and that swiftly turns to depression"
    - unhappiness, sadness, melancholy
2. melancholia, misery, sorrow, woe, gloom, despondency, low spirits despair, desolation, hopelessness, upset, tearfulness, disorder, SAD

The first thing we must do is to recognize that none of these symptoms come from God. Also, we must recognize that going into this chapter we will be looking at depression and everything that comes with it in the spirit realm. Depression is one of the Devil's main tools that he uses to destroy people from the inside out.

I touched on this subject a little in my first book, *A New Life Is Expecting You*. But right here, right now we will be diving in. I will begin with these two verses from the bible.

> 2 Timothy 1:7 KJV- For God hath not given us the spirit of fear; but of power, and of love, and of a sound mind.

Wait a minute! Did you notice? Fear is a spirit! If fear is a spirit, then what do you think misery, desolation, hopelessness, disorder, anxiety, and the rest of them are? Depression often comes in after some form of fear has set in. For example, there are different types of fear that are meant to destroy you.

For example, here are a couple more for you to consider. The *fear of rejection*, and *self-rejection*. These two bring in with them companions such as abandonment, loneliness, seclusion, hopelessness, anxiety, loneliness, and others. These unclean evil spirits do not travel alone. They carry many more destructive spirits with them. Notice this verse.

> 1 John 4:18 - There is no fear in love; but perfect love casteth out fear: because <u>fear hath torment</u>. He that feareth is not made perfect in love.

This is such an important verse in so many ways. But the phrase that pops out to me the most is, "fear hath torment." That is exactly what depression is, it's mental torment. We are going to get you some real biblical answers so you can be set free. But remember, this is new information for many people, it is to be looked at in the spiritual sense through the examples the Word of God provides for us. Jesus Christ told us that some evil spirits are stronger than others and that removing them requires prayer and fasting. Here are the Bible verses for you to see for yourself.

<u>Mark 9:17-29 KJV</u>

> 17) And one of the multitudes answered and said, Master, I have brought unto thee my son, which hath a dumb spirit.
>
> 18) And wheresoever he taketh him, he teareth him: and he foameth, and gnasheth with his teeth, and pineth away: and I spoke to thy disciples that they should cast him out; and they could not.

19) He answered him, and saith, O faithless generation, how long shall I be with you? How long shall I suffer you? Bring him unto me.

20) And they brought him unto him: and when he saw him, straightway the spirit tare him; and he fell on the ground, and wallowed foaming.

21) And he asked his father, how long is it ago this came unto him? And he said, Of a child.

22) And ofttimes it hath cast him into the fire, and into the waters, to destroy him: but if thou canst do anything, have compassion on us, and help us.

23) Jesus said unto him, if thou canst believe, all things are possible to him that believeth.

24) And straightway the father of the child cried out, and said with tears, Lord, I believe; help thou, my unbelief.

25) When Jesus saw that the people came running together, he rebuked the foul spirit, saying unto him, thou dumb and deaf spirit, I charge thee, come out of him, and enter no more into him.

26) And the spirit cried, and rent him sore, and came out of him: and he was as one dead; insomuch that many said, He is dead.

27) But Jesus took him by the hand and lifted him up; and he arose.

28) And when he was come into the house, his disciples asked him privately, why could not we cast him out?

29) And he said unto them, this kind can come forth by nothing, but by prayer and fasting.

Did you notice that verse seventeen names the characteristics of the evil spirit that was tormenting the boy? It is a spirit that causes the boy to be unable to speak. Today we would call the boy, "mentally challenged". Verse eighteen shows us how this demon torments the boy. In verse twenty-five, Jesus rebuked a demon of epileptic seizures.

Epilepsy is a demonic spirit? Do you see it now? This should light a spiritual Holy Ghost fire under you! Don't you see that you and your loved ones can be healed in Jesus' name? There is a spirit realm that is destroying people and we (the Church) are largely oblivious to what is going on because we've refused to seek God with all our hearts and souls. Also, please note verse nineteen

Jesus called them a faithless generation. In verse twenty-eight, we see that not just anyone can drive out these demons, and verse twenty says it's "because of so little faith" But in verses 28 and 29, we see that faith, prayer, and fasting are required for God to administer this miracle. Now, do you see the other side of this spiritual warfare fight taking place in the spirit world and we are in the middle of it all?

Many people around the world, even in our circles of family and friends are dealing with this horrible evil possession that most people would call a disease. They end up taking medication to subdue and tolerate it, but they never get rid of it. Through the blood of Jesus Christ, you can get rid of it forever.

The fact of the matter is that depression is an evil spirit that is on assignment to destroy you and your family. We find ourselves fighting this unwelcome demon every day. I am fully aware that so many people including "Bible scholars" will disagree with me and say that it's not a demon, but rather a disease or a sickness. And many would say that a true Christian can't have a demon of any.

Well, then to you I say, how dare you limit God's love, grace, mercy, and power? If you make the mistake of underestimating the devil's power and influence, he will tear you apart and sift your life like wheat. You must forsake all doubt and remove all boundaries to allow Jesus

Christ and the power of the Holy Spirit to work on your behalf. Jesus delivered believers (set them free) everywhere He went. Because one can't be set free if they don't believe. Jesus said in the book of Luke chapter four that He came to set the captives free. I would also be as bold as to say, "Until you have seen a demon of depression screaming and fighting its way out of a person, then keep your opinion to yourself." The fact is that you're speaking your opinion and I am speaking through personal experience as well as the guidance of The Holy Spirit.

Modern-day believers who have never been taught the power and authority given to the Church by our Lord Jesus are the problem. The Devil rules in some "Christian homes" because much of today's Church is powerless. There are so many Bible stories where God's chosen people fought and struggled with depression. Just to name a few, there was Job, King David, Hannah, and others. But one of my favorites would have to be Prophet Elijah.

Elijah was used by God like none other. He is the one in the Bible that made the axe head float after it fell into the river. He is also the prophet who took on Ahab and Jezebel who ruled Israel worshiping the god Baal.

Elijah challenged the rulers of Israel, Ahab, and Jezebel. They each built an altar to their God. Elijah said, "I will build an altar of sacrifice to my God." Then told Ahab and Jezebel to build an altar of sacrifice to their god Baal. Elijah then called for Baal's prophets to come and be a part of their ceremony as well. Four hundred and fifty of Baal's prophets were present. They agreed to cry out to their God, and Elijah would cry out to his. The god that lights the altar with fire first, will be the true God.

So, the four hundred and fifty profits of Baal that Ahab and Jezebel sent to call out to Baal failed miserably. They cried out with everything they had, dancing, shouting, praying, and begging for Baal to show up and ignite their altar with fire. Elijah stood near, saying, "Maybe you should cry louder! Maybe he can't hear you! So, they did, they cried out louder and louder. They even cut themselves with knives and lancets. But the god Baal never showed up! Then it was Elijah's turn here is the story right out of the Bible so you can see it for yourself.

1 KINGS 18:22-39

> 22) Then Elijah said to them, "I am the only one of the Lord's prophets left, but Baal has four hundred and fifty prophets.
>
> 23) Get two bulls for us. Let Baal's prophets choose one for themselves and let them cut it into pieces and put it on the wood but not set fire to it. I will prepare the other bull and put it on the wood but not set fire to it.
>
> 24) Then you call on the name of your god, and I will call on the name of the Lord. The god who answers by fire—he is God." Then all the people said, "What you say is good."
>
> 25) Elijah said to the prophets of Baal, "Choose one of the bulls and prepare it first, since there are so many of you. Call on the name of your god, but do not light the fire."
>
> 26) So they took the bull given them and prepared it.
>
> Then they called on the name of Baal from morning till noon. "Baal, answer us!" they shouted. But there was no response; no one answered. And they danced around the altar they had made.
>
> 27) At noon Elijah began to taunt them. "Shout louder!" he said. "Surely, he is a god! Perhaps he is deep in thought, or busy, or traveling. Maybe he is sleeping and must be awakened."
>
> 28) So they shouted louder and slashed themselves with swords and spears, as was their custom, until their blood flowed.

29) Midday passed, and they continued their frantic prophesying until the time for the evening sacrifice. But there was no response, no one answered, no one paid attention.

30) Then Elijah said to all the people, "Come here to me." They came to him, and he repaired the altar of the Lord, which had been torn down.

31) Elijah took twelve stones, one for each of the tribes descended from Jacob, to whom the word of the Lord had come, saying, "Your name shall be Israel."

32) With the stones he built an altar in the name of the Lord, and he dug a trench around it large enough to hold two seahs of seed.

33) He arranged the wood, cut the bull into pieces, and laid it on the wood. Then he said to them, "Fill four large jars with water and pour it on the offering and on the wood."

34) "Do it again," he said, and they did it again.

"Do it a third time," he ordered, and they did it the third time.

35) The water ran down around the altar and even filled the trench.

36) At the time of sacrifice, the prophet Elijah stepped forward and prayed: "Lord, the God of Abraham, Isaac, and Israel, let it be known today that you are God in Israel and that I am your servant and have done all these things at your command.

37) Answer me, Lord, answer me, so these people will know that you, Lord, are God, and that you are turning their hearts back again."

38) Then the fire of the Lord fell and burned up the sacrifice, the wood, the stones, and the soil, and also licked up the water in the trench.

39) When all the people saw this, they fell prostrate and cried, "The

> Lord—he is God! The Lord—he is God!"

Wow! This amazes me. The reason I decided to include this part of Elijah's story is to show that Elijah had been used by God to do miracles. He was no stranger to God's glory and power. God lit the altar with fire even after filling the trench with water. Nothing is impossible for our God.

Four hundred fifty false prophets were wiped out! God did everything! The Lord fights the battles for His people! However, in the next chapter, Elijah seemed to have little understanding of God, His glory, favor, love, and redemption.

The main reason I included this part of Elijah's story is that in many ways we are the same as Elijah. You and I have also been hand-picked and chosen by God. We've also run from the enemy. We buy into the devil's lies and we've disobeyed God. The devil's deception gets a grip on us and paralyzes us to the point of wanting to give up and fear creeps in. Even after God has proven His love for us. Think about it, take a moment to reflect on a time in your life when you have seen a miracle from God in your life. Did He heal you or someone you know from cancer or some other illness? Or did He rescue you from danger where you knew that it had to have been God that saved you? Think about it, I am sure that you remember a few times that God demonstrated His love for you and answered your prayers.

What Are You Doing Here?

Now let's move on to the next part of Elijah's journey. We have just seen that God hugely used Elijah and wiped out four hundred and fifty of Baal's prophets. Now we are about to see a mistake we all make. The enemy threatened, and Elijah gave in to fear. He ran for his life forgetting, or better yet not understanding the magnitude of what God had done for him by defeating the false prophets and proving that He and only He is the One True Living God. Let's look.

1 Kings 19 KJV

Now Ahab told Jezebel everything Elijah had done and how he had killed all the prophets with the sword.

2) So, Jezebel sent a messenger to Elijah to say, "May the gods deal with me, be it ever so severely, if by this time tomorrow I do not make your life like that of one of them."

3) Elijah was afraid and ran for his life. When he came to Beersheba in Judah, he left his servant there,

4) While he himself went on a day's journey into the wilderness. He came to a broom bush, sat down under it, and prayed that he might die. "I have had enough, Lord," he said. "Take my life; I am no better than my ancestors."

5) Then he lay down under the bush and fell asleep.

All at once an angel touched him and said, "Get up and eat."

6) He looked around, and there by his head was some bread baked over hot coals, and a jar of water. He ate and drank and then lay down again.

7) The angel of the Lord came back a second time and touched him and said, "Get up and eat, for the journey is too much for you."

8) So he got up and ate and drank. Strengthened by that food, he traveled forty days and forty nights until he reached Horeb, the mountain of God.

9) There he went into a cave and spent the night

Then the Lord Appears to Elijah

And the word of the Lord came to him: "What are you doing here,

Elijah?"

10) He replied, "I have been very zealous for the Lord God Almighty. The Israelites have rejected your covenant, torn down your altars, and put your prophets to death with the sword. I am the only one left, and now they are trying to kill me too."

11) The Lord said, "Go out and stand on the mountain in the presence of the Lord, for the Lord is about to pass by."

Then a great and powerful wind tore the mountains apart and shattered the rocks before the Lord, but the Lord was not in the wind. After the wind, there was an earthquake, but the Lord was not in the earthquake.

12) After the earthquake came to a fire, but the Lord was not in the fire. And after the fire came a gentle whisper.

13) When Elijah heard it, he pulled his cloak over his face and went out and stood at the mouth of the cave.

Then a voice said to him, "What are you doing here, Elijah?"

14) He replied, "I have been very zealous for the Lord God Almighty. The Israelites have rejected your covenant, torn down your altars, and put your prophets to death with the sword. I am the only one left, and now they are trying to kill me too."

15) The Lord said to him, "Go back the way you came, and go to the Desert of Damascus. When you get there, anoint Hazael king over Aram.

16) Also, anoint Jehu son of Nimshi king over Israel, and anoint Elisha son of Shaphat from Abel Meholah to succeed you as prophet.

17) Jehu will put to death any who escape the sword of Hazael, and Elisha will put to death any who escape the sword of Jehu.

> 18) Yet I reserve seven thousand in Israel—all whose knees have not bowed down to Baal and whose mouths have not kissed him.

A very important part of this is in verse two, we see that Jezebel, an enemy of God and Elijah, threatens Elijah. This was no empty threat, however, what we need to see here is that Jezebel is a representation of Satan, the devil.

The devil threatens God's people all day long with threats like: "Nobody loves you; God can't hear you; you will die of what your parents died of; you are going to lose everything; nobody cares about you; God can't hear you." Just like Elijah, fear sets in, and we run from God instead of running to Him.

him. Through our own misguided lives and our own decisions, we find ourselves in an unhealthy mental state. We see symptoms that were brought in by fear, anxiety, frustration, hopelessness, anger, resentment, rejection, fear of rejection, self-rejection, seclusion, and many more.

TIME FOR RESTORATION

Another part of this story that is important for us to see is in verse four.

Elijah is ready to give up, he is praying for God to take his life. He is tired of running, he is scared he feels like he has no purpose, and he also feels like he's all alone. He even says, "I'm the only one left." He is basking in his solitude, depression, and fear. He crawled into a cave. Most of us do the same thing when we are scared. We say things like, "I don't want to see anyone, or I don't want anyone to see me this way!"

Here's my favorite, "I need to deal with this MY WAY!" No, you don't need to deal with anything!

God fed Elijah bread and water. Jesus Christ tells us that He is the bread of life and that He is the living water. We need to slow down and eat. What do I mean? We need to eat the living Word of God and be filled with His Holy Spirit.

In the Bible, the Holy Spirit is referred to as Water, Wine, Blood of Jesus, Fire, Smoke, Wind, and the living Word of God. Jesus is our spiritual food.

The angel of the Lord told Elijah that he needed to eat what He provided for him because the journey was too much for him. We too are on a journey. On this journey called life, we will never regain our strength and complete the journey without Christ. We must get into His Word and apply it to our lives. The Lord told Elijah to come out of the cave and present himself on the top of the mountain. Stop hiding, stop running. You don't have to. There is freedom for you in Christ.

Elijah's misguided decisions put him there. God did not put him there. How do we know this? Because God asked him, "What are you doing here, Elijah?" God may be asking you the same thing right now. This dark place that you are in, this cave of depression, solitude, hopelessness, hurt, bitterness, fear, rejection, and abandonment. God is asking, "What are you doing here? You are my child; you don't have to hide. There is no shame in Jesus' name!" Just like God told Elijah, "Go to the top of the hill and the mouth of the cave, I will be waiting for you there." This implies the truth that you put yourself there; now you must take the initiative and make the effort to come out and the Lord will meet you halfway at the entrance.

When Elijah obeyed the Lord's instruction and stepped out, he had to cover his face because he was now in the presence of the Almighty! There is no more beautiful place to be than in the presence of God. You have God's undivided attention right now! The Lord is telling you to come out from the dead dark cave of depression. Jesus died in your place so you can have victory over these unwelcomed demons. You don't have to deal with them! The only thing you must do is to come to Him with all your heart, mind, spirit, and soul. You don't have to light any candles or say a certain prayer. Those are religious acts. Jesus told us not to be like those people. He wants to hear from your heart.

> Matthew 6:5 - "And when you pray, do not be like the hypocrites, for they love to pray standing in the synagogues and on the street corners to be seen by others. Truly I tell you, they have received their reward in full.
>
> Matthew 6:7 - And when you pray, do not use vain repetitions as the heathen does. For they think that they will be heard for their many words.

Come to Jesus with all your heart. Give Him all your burdens. Here is the best part about loving Jesus and Him loving you. He has given us His authority over all these unwelcomed evil, foul, unclean spirits. Jesus Christ is the only one who could do this for us because Jesus is the only one who died on the cross for our sins. His mother can't forgive us of our sins, Peter can't forgive us of our sins. Only Jesus shed His sinless blood for our sins. All authority in heaven and earth has been given to Him, and He has given it to those who love, believe, and live for Him.

> Matthew 28:18 - Then Jesus came to them and said, "All authority in heaven and on earth has been given to me.
>
> Then he gave His people his authority.
>
> Luke 10:19 - Behold, I give unto you power to tread on serpents and scorpions, and over all the power of the enemy: and nothing shall by any means hurt you.

Friend, this is true power! You must allow the Lord Jesus Christ to set you free; this is your time to be set free! The Lord has located you. It's time to come to Jesus Christ with all your mental, emotional, physical, and spiritual hurts and baggage, just as you are right now. Don't wait another day. Now that you have a better understanding of what you are dealing with, this is the beginning of the rest of your life. Remember, you must make a conscious effort to allow Him to change in your life. Jesus says to come as you are, but He doesn't say stay as you are. I invite you to receive Jesus into your heart to be your Lord and Savior. Believe and receive your salvation and your fresh new beginning in Christ.

Congratulations! Welcome, to your new life! I will now pray over you and show you how to pray through the verse of Luke 10:19 as well as Matthew 18:18.

> "Heavenly Father, I come to your throne in the name of Jesus, your Son, my Savior. I apply the living blood of Jesus over the one reading these words. I ask in the name of Jesus you will reveal yourself to them at this very moment. Send your Holy Spirit to comfort them and grant them your peace. In the powerful name of Jesus, and through the authority given to me by Him I bind all unclean, evil, foul spirits of depression, fear anxiety, and all their evil roots and companions. I bind you now and cast you out of this person in the name of Jesus. In the name of Jesus of Nazareth, I declare you, my reader's freedom. Mental, emotional, and physical freedom! In Jesus' name, I pray. Amen.

Matthew 18:18 - Verily I say unto you, Whatsoever ye shall bind on earth shall be bound in heaven: and whatsoever ye shall loose on earth shall be loosed in heaven.

Identify the Source

Matthew 12:29 - Or again, how can anyone enter a strong man's house and carry off his possessions unless he first ties up the strong man? Then he can plunder his house.

The strongman Jesus is talking about is the head demon in charge that is commanding the others as they execute their evil plan against you and your family. In this case, the head demon in charge would be depression. However, we need to examine ourselves to see what caused the depression. What opened the door for that demon to enter?

Did someone hurt your feelings or offend you? Did someone close to you die too soon? Were your love and trust betrayed? Ask yourself, take yourself back. What caused this depression? There you will find the strongman.

Now "the house" Jesus refers to is you. The devils call our bodies their house. However, once we come to Christ our body becomes the temple of the Holy Spirit. You will spoil his "goods and tie him up by binding him" in the name of Jesus. This is how you strip away the devil's rights from your mind, body, spirit, and soul.

In closing: Write down all your mental, emotional, and physical issues. Try to narrow them down to what caused this depression. Let's get to the source of the problem. First, cover yourself in the blood of Jesus, then remember that the name of Jesus is your authority. Now, one by one bind them in the name of Jesus, then cast them all out! Everything must be done with a clean heart before the Lord, and it will only be effective if it is done in Jesus' name. Command them to go in Jesus' name. Take authority and speak with confidence in Jesus' name.

Welcome to your freedom! This my friend is true power! Jesus makes all things new. Allow the Lord to repair your shattered heart. Know that you are deeply loved. I invite you now to come to Jesus and pray this prayer with me, I will take you by the hand and place your hands in the hands of Jesus. Let's pray this prayer to the Lord.

Prayer of Salvation

> Heavenly Father, I come to you in the name of Jesus. I know that I am a sinner. I believe in your Son, my Savior Jesus Christ.
>
> Jesus, come into my heart and forgive all my sins. I believe you died on the cross for me and arose three days later so I might be set free and live with you forever. Be my Lord, be my Savior from this moment one of. In Jesus's name, I pray, Amen.

Chapter 6

The Real You

As I was growing up, I was always told to love the Lord. But nobody ever told me how to Love the Lord. I was always told things like, "You need to forgive" but nobody ever told me how to forgive. I was even told, "You need to just forgive yourself, so God can bless you." but nobody ever showed me how to forgive myself.

What I discovered after so many years of being lost and emotionally upside down was that I didn't have to fix myself or even find myself before coming to God. I had to come to God exactly the way I was. I didn't have to fix my condition or situation first. What I had to do was offer "what I was" to God. I had to be honest with myself as to, "what I was" not who I was but "What I was." I had to come to terms with the understanding that I am a sinner, a liar, a thief, a fornicator, a drunk, a drug addict, a coward, a hateful bitter person and so much more. Not just recognizing that I had a problem but also recognizing that in my situation I was the problem.

My mother once said to me, "you need to give yourself to God." Those words still ring in my head. I knew she was right but again. How can I offer myself to God in all honesty, if I don't know who I am? I know what I believe, but like most people, I don't know why I believe it. I knew that I was a sinner, I knew all the bad stuff about myself but deep down inside of myself I didn't know who I was. I felt that I needed to find out, I needed truth, I needed confirmation, needed to be sure that God would accept the real me. For the first time in my life, I wanted to be real about something and I wanted to make my life count for something. I at least needed to know what I was offering to God.

I felt as if every time I had ever prayed to God and opened my heart to the Lord. I was offering "The Me" that I had invented. A false make-believe version of myself. But the truth is that God can't love a false version of you. Because, as long, as we are in denial of the simple fact that we are sinners and we are still living in that sin, we are allowing a wall to disconnect us from God and all his grace and mercy. This prevents him from working in our lives. It isn't until we come to a place of complete honesty with ourselves, and with God, and recognize what we are, that the Holy Spirit can reveal more of ourselves that needs to change. Little by little the things that were once so important to you all of the sudden won't be and one day you will start to lose interest in the old things that would once drive and motivate you. These old things will slowly pass away you will start to have a new direction.

So, once again I found myself going to the bible for answers. Since I knew that I was the problem I knew that I had to start with the true source of the problem, "Me." I was so full of self-hatred. I hated myself for all the wrong that I had caused my family, my friends, and myself. I had to figure out a way to forgive myself for every wrong and every lie I had ever committed. Here I was again finding myself searching for the solution. I had to ask myself, "How can I forgive others if I can't even forgive myself? How can I ask God to accept me if I can't even accept myself?" It was at that moment when I truly asked myself this question, "What can fix hate?" The answer was Love.

One day while I was praying, I remember talking with God as if I could hear his voice. I can clearly remember that conversation, God was telling me to love myself the way he loved me. I need to Love myself. Are you kidding me, Lord? I don't even like the way I look! I don't even like myself! How am I supposed to love myself the way you love me if I don't even know how you love me? I know that you love me very much because you died for me on the cross. But Lord, I don't know how or why you could love such a worthless man as myself, I am not worthy of your love, or your grace and mercy.

The year was around 1999 when God showed me that I was capable of loving someone. This was a few years before I even met my wife and had a family of my own. God was showing me that I wasn't as cold-hearted as I thought I was because God asked me these simple questions. Do you love your mother? I answered, "Yes" do you love your father? I answered, "Yes" and then God showed me his greatest commandment.

Matthew 22:36-39 – KJV

> 36) "Teacher, which is the greatest commandment in the Law?"
>
> 37) Jesus replied: "Love the Lord your God with all your heart and with all you soul and with all your mind.
>
> 38) This is the first and greatest commandment.
>
> 39) And the second is like it: Love your neighbor as yourself.

Wow! I always knew that I was supposed to love the Lord with everything in my inner being. But the words I had been searching for my entire life were looking right back at me and I couldn't avoid those words, it's like the words took on a life of themselves. They were like a sharp blade piercing right through my soul. Also, God said that I am supposed to love my neighbor as "myself." That old saying is so true, you know the one that says, "You can't love someone if you can't love yourself" because you can't offer what you're not capable of having. By the time, I reached this point in my life, I am finally realizing that I do have love inside of me, Wow! I am capable of loving someone! This is great news to me because I do love my parents and I do love God. I now know that I have a starting point to be able to change my life around. I now know that if I can love them, then I can be loved. If I can forgive myself and others, then I am also able to be forgiven by

God and by others.

> Romans 5:8 KJV - But God shows his love for us in that while we were still sinners, Christ died for us.

This bible verse tells me that while I was still feeling lost and living in sin, God first reached out to me in love, while Christ died for me. Friend, all of this applies to you too. No matter what you are going through in your life right now at this moment you don't have to fix your situation first. You can come to Christ with all your fears, failures, worries, hurts doubts and so much more. His mercy is more than enough for us. Well, as I mentioned before I was searching for answers from the Lord and the best place to hear from God is through his word. Then the Lord spoke to my heart by giving me this bible verse.

> Ephesians 2:4-5 - But God, being rich in mercy, because of the great love with which he loved us, even when we were dead in our trespasses, made us alive together with Christ.

I finally see it! Do you? There is nothing that we can do to earn God's love. He already loves us since the beginning of time. Taking a step back and focusing deeply for a moment on Jesus Christ and having a fundamental understanding of what he did for us on the cross. We need to understand that His mercy and his great love for us, came through his obedience to God the Father. His obedience and love for the father are what saved us. It's because of his love that I can walk through life with confidence knowing that Jesus Christ is with me. Not because of who I am, but because of who he is in me. I realized that if Christ can bear my sins as his own and die for me, and then forgive me of all my sins, I should be able to forgive myself and others. It is because Christ is God in the flesh and is bigger than I am and since Christ is offering forgiveness to us for every sin that we have ever committed as well as our rebellion against God. Then we should be able to accept his forgiveness and be able to forgive ourselves for all our wrongs and mistakes.

Friend, don't you see? All of this that I went through applies to you as well. There is plenty of God's grace for all of us. The bible verse we read earlier tells us that God is rich in mercy. This is where we can find our mental and emotional rest. Knowing that we can come to him with everything and rest in his arms. Now we can offer him the real you. That means good or bad, offer it all to him finding assurance, and knowing that he will accept you exactly the way you are, takes away all the pressure in thinking that we should present ourselves perfectly to God. We don't have to come to him with ourselves fixed first, once you can absorb this reality as your own, then you can start to function as your true self that God intended you to be in him and live through him.

Please know that the rules that society has taught us growing up about being accepted, do not apply when it comes to God. The beauty of it all is that we don't have to try to earn God's love because there is nothing that we could do to earn it. He already loves you, his love is his grace and we are undeserving of his grace. The beauty of his grace is that he extends it to us anyway because of his love for us.

The best thing that you could ever do for yourself is to examine your life right now and take everyone that you know, along with everything that you know to be your life out of the equation. Here is an exercise that will help, follow these instructions. Grab yourself a sheet of paper. Write "God" in the center of the circle. Give yourself plenty of space to create categories with God in the center of your paper.

Step #1 Draw a big circle on a sheet of paper.

Step #2 In the center of that paper list your priorities.

Step #3 List all the important people in your life.

Step #4 List three things that are most important to you.

Step #5 Note where you spend most of your time.

Step #6 How/where do you spend most of your money?

Step#7 Now cross off the least important in all categories.

Step #8 Now cross off the three least important in each category.

Step #9 Now cross off all the rest of the least important in all categories. But leave "only one most important thing in your life"

What is it?

Step #10 Your circle should consist of only you and God.

Because when your life is over here on earth, it is just going to be you standing before God. Then what?

Teach your family to love and respect each other, teach your babies everything you know about God, and live your life to the fullest, with no regrets, but when it's all over, here on earth, it's going to be you standing in front of the Lord. The choice that you made about Christ will now determine where you are going to spend eternity. Jesus will be looking in your eyes, piercing your soul with love. It is only you and Jesus Christ and you're looking back at him. How do you feel? What are you going to say to him? Now at this very moment is your chance to talk with the Lord and tell him how you feel. Have you decided to follow Jesus? Are you living for Him now? Go ahead stop reading, mark this page and put the book down, and tell the Lord how you feel. Unload your heart along with every burden and desire. Tell him everything!

Well, how did it go? I hope you put the book down and talked to the Lord. You will feel unexplainable freedom if you did this with all your heart. If you did do it without thinking you feel silly or what if someone walks in and sees me? If you did this with a true hunger for freedom, then you just made the first step toward knowing who you are. Congratulations on taking a real step in getting to know the real you and welcome to the first day of real spiritual freedom. This is the real you, it's a true feeling of liberation. A feeling of not caring what others think and releasing the old self by doing something you normally wouldn't do. Releasing yourself into the Lord's care is such a peaceful feeling. We as human beings wonder what our true purpose in life is and wonder who can give us real direction, with real concern and love with no ulterior motive. God did this for us in the following bible verse.

<u>Jeremiah 29:11-14 KJV</u>

> 11) For I know the plans I have for you," declares the Lord, "plans to prosper you and not to harm you, plans to give you hope and a future.
>
> 12) Then you will call on me and come and pray to me, and I will listen to you.
>
> 13) You will seek me and find me when you seek me with all your heart.
>
> 14) I will be found by you," declares the Lord, "and will bring you back from captivity. I will gather you from all the nations and places where I have banished you," declares the Lord, "and will bring you back to the place from which I carried you into exile."

God is talking to you right here in this verse, he is also giving you instruction and direction for your life. God is also giving you a promise that he is going to free you from your old self and all your emotional baggage. Friend, just let him truly be the center of your life. Let today be the first day of the rest of your life in Christ.

If you will, take time to read those verses again and you will see the purpose for your life. The first plan that God has for you is for you to seek him with all your heart in verse thirteen. The next thing that you will see, is a promise to you in verse fourteen, "that he will be found by you." God isn't hiding from us but we must be the ones that need to seek him with all our hearts. The next promise you will see is that "he will bring you back from captivity," there is your freedom! Mental, Emotional, Spiritual, Physical, Financial, whatever your deep need is he promises to bring you out of it and make your life whole as he intended your life to be in him and with him, and through him.

The Lord promises to bring us out of captivity, don't you see that many people today as well as believers in Christ Jesus are captives in our minds? Many of us are praising God from within the prison of our minds and emotions, so many of us are still allowing unforgiveness to rule over us and restrain us from our blessings as well as healing. It is one thing to be healed and another thing to be made whole.

Healing is almost always physical, but to be made whole is when your spirit, your body, and your soul re-align as God intended you to be. You must remember that when God created man, He created spirit, body, and soul, so when these three are out of alignment from within your inner being, this is when confusion, anxiety, depression, and mental chaos can rule in a person's life, so in the name of Jesus Christ we must command these three within us to re-align as God intended for you to be. Remember that God is the God of ALL spirits including yours. When you decree and declare this in His name your inner spirit man must obey the name of Jesus Christ.

The real you is in Christ, He is waiting for your will(desires) to line up with his will (desires) for your life. This will be the meeting place where God will introduce you to the real you. Once you disagree with every plan that the enemy has against you and agree with the will of God. You are then about to receive your breakthrough. Trust in Him with all your heart, with every fiber of your being surrender to the Lord. Blessings await you today.

Congratulations your new life has just begun. Welcome to the real you.

LEANDRO OLIVAREZ

Chapter 7

POWER

Definition: pow·er

The ability to do something or act in a particular way, especially as a faculty or quality.

Synonyms:

- Ability, capacity, capability, potential, potentiality, faculty, property, competence, competency, the capacity, or ability to direct or influence the behavior of others or the course of events.
- Influence, authority, weight, sway, control, say, ascendancy, dominance, advantage, pressure, edge, standing, prestige, rank, weightage.
- Physical strength and force exerted by something or someone: "The power of the storm"
- Strength, powerfulness, might, force, forcefulness, mightiness.

The word that best describes power is *love*, and through love comes *authority*. If you have the authority to act and speak in a certain way to display the love of God this is the true power that gives us dominion over something or even someone. This is true power, to be able to make an impact on a person that could change their life. People all around us are looking for tangible answers for their lives in today's day and age. The problem we come across is that people need direction, most people don't know what their inner spirit is longing for. They are fully aware that there is some type of void in their lives, but most can't quite put their finger on what exactly it is that they are longing for, and the very reason for this is that most people are not conscious of the spirit world that is all around us. The goal of this chapter is to enlighten you to see that true power is not success. Here is why in the spirit realm success does not intimidate Satan or any demon. You can flaunt your success all you want, but that is not power! True power is in the name that is above all names, the name of Jesus Christ. This name changes atmospheres and breathes life into those who are burnt out with life. His name raises the dead. His name commands angels to move on your behalf. His name is POWER!

Know that you were created for a greater purpose, I will be bold enough to say that if you have been living your life without Jesus Christ and a personal relationship with His Holy Spirit, then you have not even tapped into your greater purpose yet. Your greater purpose is what you were put on this earth for as you give Him the glory every step of the way. You will find that when you discover the real you and begin to live according to the direction of the Holy Spirit in your everyday life, this is where you will find everything that you have been longing for.

When you begin to live in the purpose you were created for, your attitude will change towards others, as well as yourself, you will display inner peace and assurance of knowing exactly who you are and who Christ is in you. Knowing your identity is crucial for success and happiness. Let me ask you a question: Have you ever known a happy person who doesn't even know who they are? I don't think so. Confidence comes through identity, and we find our identity in Christ. We use the love of God as a weapon to combat the enemy to go to places to reach the lost and the broken-hearted. We use the power of love for humanity and we use our spiritual authority to bind and cast out the demons that are tormenting people. Jesus commissioned us to get out there and set the captives free!

Once you know your identity in Christ, He will give you authority to bear His name and by faith, you will be able to move mountains and sleigh Giants. Mountains and giants are obstacles in the spirit realm that will get in your way, but through Christ, you will have the Authority to move them all with the mention of His name.

Jesus Christ was given from God the Father all Authority / Power in all of heaven and earth and under the earth.

Matthew 28:16-19 KJV

16) Then the eleven disciples went away into Galilee, into a mountain where Jesus had appointed them.

17) And when they saw him, they worshipped him: but some doubted.

18) And Jesus came and spake unto them, saying, all power is given unto me in heaven and in earth.

19) Go ye therefore, and teach all nations, baptizing them in the name of the Father, and of the Son, and of the Holy Ghost:

Do you see it? Verse 18, Our Lord has all authority over the world as well as the spirit realm. But look at the next verse, He says to "go and teach all people, and baptize them in the Name of The Father, the Son, and the Holy Ghost." The Lord is saying to go and do this in His Name. He is saying for us to go and change lives, change atmospheres, in His name.

So, think about the Lord Jesus, through His death and His resurrection was given all power; which means all authority. All means ALL! There is nothing left after all. It all belongs to Him. True power is His! There is power in His holy name. All power, all dominion, all authority over the spirit world, and the natural world, which means that since our God is the God of all spirits, all spirits are subject to His name.

The Bible tells us that His name is above all other names.

<u>Philippians 2:9-11 KJV</u>

> 9) Wherefore God also hath highly exalted him, and given him a name which is above every name:
>
> 10) That at the name of Jesus every knee should bow, of things in heaven, and things in earth, and things under the earth.
>
> 11) And that every tongue should confess that Jesus Christ is Lord, to the glory of God the Father.

I know that you see it too. Jesus' name is above every name. God the Father has highly exalted our Lord. Every knee should bow (show reverence) to things of heaven and things on the earth and things under the earth. I hope you are receiving this. Through Jesus Christ, we are commissioned to bear His name, His name means salvation, and His name is a title. His name is authority. Here is the best part for you and me. The baptism of the Holy Spirit and His fire allows us to represent Him in both the spirit realm and the natural realm.

> Luke 10:19 KJV - Behold, I give unto you power to tread on serpents and scorpions, and over all the power of the enemy: and nothing shall by any means hurt you.

Authority is power. Jesus was given ALL power. Then He gave that same power to His Bride, "the Church." This is true power. You are spiritually legally authorized to change the plans of demons and the plans of Satan. This is the power of the Holy Spirit that is given to the Church. And the Devil is not allowed to retaliate. "Nothing shall by any means hurt you." Allow me to break this down for you. Now that you accepted Jesus Christ to be your Lord and Savior, the Lord Jesus deposits inside of you His Holy Spirit. He is God's gift to us. And He dwells inside of us. The Bible says that "Know ye not that you are the temple of the Holy Ghost?" He is in you; He is your comforter; He is your teacher as well as your protector. He responds to your faith in Him.

The Holy Spirit does not come empty-handed. John the Baptist said the following:

> Matthew 3:11KJV - I indeed baptize you with water unto repentance. but he that cometh after me is mightier than I, whose shoes I am not worthy to bear he shall baptize you with the Holy Ghost, and with fire:

This baptism of the Holy Spirit is necessary for the Church today. Every believer should be governed by the Holy Spirit. This is true power, which is far beyond what the corporate world teaches: "Knowledge is power," which is a half-truth. The actual truth is "Applied knowledge is power." If one lacks the Holy Spirit, they cannot apply mental knowledge to move mountains and change atmospheres. One cannot display this kind of power without the baptism of the Holy Spirit, which is also known as the anointing of the Holy Spirit. The fire that comes from the baptism of the Holy Spirit is moved by your faith. These are known as the nine gifts of the Spirit of God.

1 Corinthians 12:4-11 KJV

> 4) Now there are diversities of gifts, but the same Spirit.
>
> 5) And there are differences of administrations, but the same Lord.
>
> 6) And there are diversities of operations, but it is the same God which worketh all in all.
>
> 7) But the manifestation of the Spirit is given to every man to profit

> withal.
>
> 8) For to one is given by the Spirit the word of wisdom, to another the word of knowledge by the same Spirit.
>
> 9) To another faith by the same Spirit; to another the gifts of healing by the same Spirit.
>
> 10) To another the working of miracles; to another prophecy; to another discerning of spirits; to other divers' kinds of tongues; to another the interpretation of tongues:
>
> 11) But all these worketh that one and the selfsame Spirit, dividing to every man severally as he will.

This, my friend, is the true power that every believer in Christ Jesus should manifest. Jesus is our authority, His name is our power. There is power in the name of Jesus. Be baptized by the Holy Spirit. His anointing is a commission. When the Lord calls you to step into your calling, He will anoint you to carry out your mission. He will not only send you, but through His Holy Spirit, He will be with you every step of the way. My friend, step out in your faith in Christ with the assurance that He is with you, and do not be afraid because you are legally authorized to represent Him and use His Name.

> Matthew 16:19 KJV - And I will give unto thee the keys of the kingdom of heaven: and whatsoever thou shalt bind on earth shall be bound in heaven: and whatsoever thou shalt loose on earth shall be loosed in heaven.

This is the power of God to His Church. This is when you step out in faith and pull people out of their depression, anxiety, fear, rejection, fear of rejection, self-rejection, and addictions. You can display the love and the power of God and step into the authority God has given you. Work out your salvation and make sure that you are a member of the Body of Christ, "the Church"

Everything you long for in your life, you already have if you are in Christ. The Holy Spirit may be an ember in your inner spirit, but when you submit to the Lord's will in your life, He will breathe on that ember and the Holy Spirit will engulf the flame in you. Your life will never be the same after you taste the goodness, the Glory of God. I encourage you to step into the true power of God that comes from his Holy Spirit. Ask the Lord to baptize you in His Spirit.

You should know that water baptism is an outward expression representing the remission of your sins. When you go under the water that represents the grave where you bury your old life. When you come up out of the water, that represents a resurrection. It's your testimony that you are now a new person in Christ.

Now, the baptism of the Holy Spirit is when the Holy Spirit is fully in you. You are filled with Him, and out of your belly shall flow rivers of living water. Ask Him to fill you with Himself and His fire. He is not only available to you, but He is also waiting to hear from you. May the Lord be the center of your plans and dreams, and may He bless you in all you do. Remember, the true power of God is available to every believer in Jesus Christ. The power He gives His Church is to love, to love Him more, and to display His love to sinners, those who are lost without Him. When they experience the supernatural love they see in you, they will want to know Him.

LEANDRO OLIVAREZ

Chapter 8

Decree and Declare

Many today are hungry for power, and they live their lives chasing after things like money, status, big houses, cars, and such. Jesus Christ is power, and a relationship with Christ is powerful. The Bible tells us that there is power in the tongue. With your tongue, you can build someone up or tear someone down. We should always build people up, no matter what. We don't know the personal struggles of everyone. What if the person we were rude to this morning has been contemplating suicide? What if they prayed last night, "Lord, if you care, or if you're even real, then send me a sign that you hear me and love me, but if I don't hear from you, that's it. I'm done." Then their encounter with you "a Christian" was judgmental and degrading. How do you think that would make our Lord feel? Remember, we represent Him.

> Proverbs 18:21 KJV - Death and life are in the power of the tongue: and they that love it shall eat the fruit thereof.

It is very important to speak life into people. Words are like fruit. If you were to tell me I was no good, and would never accomplish anything in my life, when I was in a vulnerable state, discouraged, mentally and emotionally weak, and I believed your words, it would be as if I were eating fruit you were feeding me. The words coming out of your mouth at this point are toxic like the forbidden fruit Eve ate in the Garden of Eden. You have a choice to be the "someone" maybe you did not have in your life.

Perhaps you always wished you had someone to encourage you growing up. Maybe you wish you would have had someone directing your path. Maybe you wished you would have had someone who believed in you and would have expressed interest in you, and invested time with you. It is too easy to take the low road and be negative. Let's take a closer look at what God said to Adam and Eve.

> Genesis 2:16, 17 KJV - And the Lord God commanded the man, saying, of every tree of the garden thou mayest freely eat: 17 But of the tree of the knowledge of good and evil, thou shalt not eat of it: for in the day that thou eat thereof thou shalt surely die.

Satan himself was the forbidden fruit that was on the tree of knowledge of good and evil and his words of doubt penetrated the ears and soul of Eve to the point of her doubting everything that God said to her and Adam and for her to question God. The words of Satan became the fruit Eve ate. She didn't eat "from" it, she ate "of" it.

Words are powerful, be very careful how you choose your words. Through Christ, we can change the outcome of certain situations. According to Scripture, the way to do this is to declare and to decree. Let's get to the truth of it. Are you ready for your life to change? Let's go!

To Declare and To Decree

Decree = an official order issued by a legal authority, order, command, rule, dictate

Therefore, a decree needs to be based on God's Word..

> Matthew 28:18 (KJV) - And Jesus came and spoke unto them, saying, all power is given to me in heaven and in earth.

In another Bible translation, the word "power" is translated as the word "authority." When you take a closer look at the word "power," the Hebrew definition is government, force, rule, authority, administration, strength, and might.

When you decree in the name of Jesus Christ, your prayers become official orders in the spirit realm, and your decree should agree and line up with the Word of God. The Lord will always honor His Word and His will. Remember that a decree is a command and official order. Decrees create and make atmospheres change in both the spirit and the physical realm. A decree must be based on God's will and His intention. His purpose must be fulfilled, and are to render to Him all the honor and glory.

When I pray, the first thing I do is surrender to the Holy Spirit as I address in the spirit realm every monitoring demon, *"I bind up every foul and unclean spirit, I bind you in the name of Jesus Christ."* I also do this before I preach. When you bind evil spirits in the name of Jesus, they must obey, because every living thing is subject to the name of Jesus Christ. I want to show this to you in the Scripture.

Psalm 2:1-7 KJV

> 1) Why do the heathen rage, and the people imagine a vain thing?

The Hebrew word for "imagine" is *hagah*, which is the same word used for meditating on a thought. The nations surrounding Israel were meditating on how they were going to destroy and attack God's anointed people. This is also known in the scriptures as "The council of the wicked" that are planning their attacks against God's church. We are individually members of the body of Christ and when we gather corporately, we are in unity as the body of Christ.

> 2) The kings of the earth set themselves, and the rulers take counsel together, against the Lord, and against his anointed, saying,

Do you see this? This council sets themselves against the Lord our God, the "Anointed One", Jesus Christ. The word used for "anointed" is *Mashiyach* and this shows us that His name is more of a title that is used to identify Christ Jesus. The band of the Holy Spirit binds the enemy with these spiritual cords, and when you take your spiritual position as an active member of the Lord's Body, as a spiritual sniper for Jesus, and effective prayer warrior. These demons cannot break free from your official order for them to be bound in His name.

> 3) Let us break their bands asunder and cast away their cords from us.

Did you catch that in verse 3? They counsel with each other to try to figure out how they can break free from your decree to bind them. Therefore, we must remain in the Lord and resist sin, because when we give in to sin, we lose our spirit grip on these demons.

> 4) He that sitteth in the heavens shall laugh: the Lord shall have them in derision. Whoever said that our Lord does not have a sense of humor as He laughs at the enemy? The word derision is contemptuous ridicule or mockery, The Lord will have them in Legal contempt and ridicule them, As He laughs at them.
>
> 5) Then shall he speak unto them in his wrath and vex them in his sore displeasure.
>
> 6) Yet have I set my king upon my holy hill of Zion.
>
> 7) I will declare the decree: the Lord hath said unto me, thou art my son; this day have I begotten thee.

I hope you noticed that David declared the decree of the Lord, it is important to note that the decree of the Lord concerning David was that He would be anointed as King. When you agree with what God has said about you, the Lord will honor His Word., This is how the Word of the Lord is a double-edged sword, a weapon, The Lord speaks, and the Word is sharp, and when you agree with the Word and speak what God has written, this gives the Word its double edge. We see this in the book of Samuel.

> 2 Samuel 5:7 KJV - Therefore, now let your hands be strengthened, and be ye valiant, for your master Saul is dead, and the house of Judah have anointed me King over them.

David later fulfilled this prophecy. He constructed a tent on Mount Zion bringing the Ark of The Covenant to Jerusalem and giving a home to the decree in what he had prepared. Agree with what God has written concerning His promises to His Church. When you feel like you are losing in life, remember God's promises and allow the blood of Jesus to speak for you. This is how you begin, with a declaration. The declaration comes first it is your verbal agreement with the Word of God. The Hebrew word for declare is *achvah*, which means "to make known", or to set forth an accounting. When you declare a decree, you are speaking in authority, to make known in the spirit realm the living Word of God. You are setting the word forth in motion as a legal authority. Understand, your words release and commission angels to act on your behalf. This true power, my friend, is far beyond the fundamentals of corporate success.

> Psalm 103:20 KJV - Bless the Lord, ye his angels, that excel in strength, that do his commandments, hearkening unto the voice of his word.

Friend, recognize the power in your words. Angels that do the Lord's commands listen to the voice of His Word. It does not say that they listen for the voice "of the Lord," but it says that they listen to the voice of "His Word". You are the voice of His Word. Agree with and speak His Word. In declaring the decree of the Lord, angels are released commissioned to carry out the Lord's Word which you have spoken. See the power and the authority given to you by God?

Do not be afraid to represent the Lord in your prayers with your words. Be in covenant with The Lord, be in fasting with the Lord, be in worship. Open yourself to the Holy Spirit. Remember, you are His temple, and He resides inside you. He will be with you everywhere you go and in everything you do. Remember to declare, to make known, to set in motion. That is the official order issued by your legal authority commissioned by Jesus Christ. Never talk to the Devil. Talk AT him! Be sure to command those evil forces to abort their mission because their assignment is canceled in the name of Jesus Christ. They must obey your decree in the name of Jesus Christ.

Job 22:27 KJV

> 27) Thou shalt make thy prayer unto him, and he shall hear thee, and thou shalt pay thy vows.
>
> 28) Thou shalt also decree a thing, and it shall be established unto thee: and the light shall shine upon thy ways.

Remember this when you pray for your family, declare what God has said to you and your family according to His promises that are written for the Church, the active body of Christ. Look at it this way: Everyone has a destiny already written for them before they were born. The Devil comes in with his demons to rewrite your destiny. This is a form of forgery according to God's word. When you learn what is written concerning you and your loved ones, and the promises of the Lord that are made for you, you will be able to step in with the authority that the Lord has given His church and cancel every demonic intention, demonic plan, and every word of judgment that has been spoken against you and your family. You can then declare the goodness, mercy, and favor that is written in the book of remembrance in heaven concerning you and your bloodline. When you declare and decree the Lord's Word, Satan loses. The Lord's righteousness will shine upon you.

Friend, be active in the Lord and start praying decrees in the name of the Lord. Never forget that these are official legal orders in the spirit realm. Make your prayers cause the angels to rejoice and put the kingdom of darkness on notice that they should think twice about coming against you and your loved ones because at your spoken decree of the Lord will unleash warring angels on your behalf. Dear friend, walk in the confidence of personally knowing the Creator of heaven and earth. He knows you by name.

LEANDRO OLIVAREZ

Chapter 9

Casting All Your Cares

A few years ago, my wife and I were going through some tough times financially. Some of our struggles didn't seem to make sense in the natural but looking back at everything in spiritual terms, they all have made perfect sense. Currently, the Lord wants me to open this very personal time in our lives for you to know that you are not the only one who has faced hard times. People around the world deal with challenging times. This is the main reason I have decided to share my story with you. The reason I will share this with you is to be obedient to the Holy Spirit and to give God all the glory and honor.

Now here is what would seem strange in the natural. I have never been able to find my place in this world as far as my career goes. I have had some pretty awesome opportunities to earn a living. However, things just never worked out for me financially. The strange thing is that the Lord has always come through for us, and we have lacked nothing. The Lord has supplied our every financial need but that doesn't mean that it has been easy. It also goes deeper than just financial hardships; it's been finding my place to fit in with friends and relatives.

Don't get me wrong. I have some awesome friends and family. I am talking about fitting in and being part of a social group of people that look forward to seeing you, and with whom you have things in common. I have never found my place in this world to where I could say that this is where I belong.

There was a few years when we owned our own business. We had a sole proprietorship through a bread company. Here is the way it worked. I would place an order a week in advance for the grocery stores. Once the order arrived the next week, I would make my deliveries and tend to the product rotation on the stores' shelves.

At the end of each week, I received a paycheck based on the amount of product that had been sold off the store shelves. It was 100% Commission sales. I would count the product that had not sold, and trash it. However, I still had to pay for it. It would come out of my next week's check.

Well, the company ended up selling out to another company out of Mexico, so the corporate managers decided to charge us for all inventory because they needed to "clear their books." This went on for a couple of months so what happened to our paycheck? Suddenly, instead of getting a paycheck at the end of the week, I began receiving a bill from the company. One week I would owe the company several hundred dollars, and my check would be something like one hundred dollars. Then the next week, I'd not receive a paycheck at all. This went on for weeks at a time. Keep in mind that I still had to work, and the company kept telling me, "Everything will be okay next week. You will receive a good check, and it will balance out by then." That was a lie! I still had to put fuel in the bread truck, at least $150.00 per week, because I also ran out of town two times per week.

During this time, I would be praying for the Lord to make everything right in our finances. I was blaming the Devil for robbing us of our finances. I was at the point of getting angry with the Devil. I was binding and rebuking the Devil all day long. I couldn't understand what was happening. I would even fast for God to give me some direction. I couldn't hold on to this job any longer and we were already behind on all our bills. Christmas time was approaching. I cried out to God in my work truck asking Him, "Why, God? Why is this happening to us?" I couldn't understand why God would allow the Devil to do this to us. I was feeling heartbroken and disappointed. I wasn't blaming God, but I just didn't understand what was happening. Little did I know that the Lord was about to speak to me.

One night while I was sleeping, I had a dream. In this dream, there were three loaves of bread. One loaf was made of barley, another of wheat, and another of grains and flour, was a golden color. One had a pentagram on the packaging, and the other was in a black package. This is what the Lord showed me the loaves of bread meant through these Bible verses.

> The one loaf with the pentagram on it is a loaf of wickedness. Proverbs 4:17, They eat the bread of wickedness and drink the wine of violence.
>
> The all-black loaf is the loaf of deceit. Proverbs 20:17
>
> Food gained by fraud tastes sweet, but one ends up with a mouth full of gravel.
>
> The golden loaf of grains and flour. Leviticus 2:1, 2
>
> 1) When anyone brings a grain offering to the Lord, their offering is to be of the finest flour. They are to pour olive oil on it, put incense on it
>
> 2) and take it to Aaron's sons the priest. The priest shall take a hand full of the flour and oil, together with all the incense, and burn this as a memorial portion on the altar, a food offering, an aroma pleasing the Lord.

When I sat down to tell you about this, the Lord reminded me that I had the dream seven years ago. The other thing He wanted me to recognize was that the number seven represents completion. That itself was telling me that it was time for my family and me to move into God's favor. The Lord was telling me that the people around me that do not know Him are spiritually eating from the two unclean loaves, of wickedness and deceit. God told me that He would feed me the bread of life being Jesus Christ, and I am to feed His people and those who do not know Jesus Christ. Jesus is the good bread of life.

> John 6:35 - Jesus answered unto them I am the bread of life: he that cometh to me shall never hunger and he that believeth on me shall never thirst.

I should take my time when preparing spiritual food for the lost sheep and first dedicate every message (of food) to the Lord so that it is pleasing to Him before serving. The Lord also told me in these words, "Stop giving the Devil credit for what I am trying to do in your life. I am trying to close this door to open a bigger and better door for you. When I shut this door, do not try to reopen it, for what I shut no one can open. When I open the next, no one can shut it. I saw the verse in my dream."

> Isaiah 22:22 KJV - I will place on his shoulder the key of the house of David: what he opens no one can shut, and what he shuts no one can open.
>
> Revelation 3:7 KJV - "To the angel of the church in Philadelphia write: These are the words of him who is holy and true, who holds the key of David. What he opens no one can shut, and what he shuts no one can open.

My wife and I agreed, recognizing what was happening, and that God was in control. It has been a series of doors that God has been opening for us to walk through with Him guiding the way. It always seems as though God sends me to the places where people are struggling the most with spiritual and emotional issues. We had to step out in faith and learn to trust the Lord was going to take care of us, and that He would provide for all our family's needs. God told us to trust Him with all our hearts and our and that He would sustain us. He said that He would hold us in his hands. He has been faithful. God has repeatedly proven Himself. I can honestly say that it's not easy learning to trust Him. But when you do finally decide to let go and allow Him to be God of your life it is so worth it. I know what it's like when you feel like you might lose everything that you have worked so hard for. I understand that it can feel like you just got the air kicked out of you and it becomes a struggle to just keep on breathing. I would see these pastors showboating on TV misrepresenting God, doing it all for money and publicity, while we true pastors are living by faith and trusting in the Lord for guidance, struggling to keep the house and keep the lights on all while doing our best to raise godly children and practice what we preach.

The Lord must be our anchor all the time not just when the storms of life come rushing through. I understand the meaning of living by faith and trusting in God and waiting for His timing. I know that it's not an easy thing to do. But it's an amazing feeling when you start having a real relationship with God through Jesus Christ up close and in person. It is the most complete feeling you will ever have when He comes rushing in and begins pushing all the hurt and worry out of your mind and heart.

His Word is alive and breathing. It is so awesome to see His Word come to life and carry you and your family to a whole new level just by trusting in Him. We need to stand by every Word of His. I love the verse He gave me in a dream as if it were being handed to me on a glowing plaque, in a golden frame. This is what it read.

> 1 Peter 5:7 - Casting *all* your care upon him, for he careth for you.

Now friend, let's talk about you. I may not know you or your situation but right now as you are reading this book, know that God wants you to trust Him. He will help you in your time of need. He understands everything you are going through in your life right now. He also understands how hard it can be to take that step of faith. But everything we do should be by faith. I hold on to those words that keep ringing in my head, "If you would only believe, you would see the glory of God!"

The Lord wants you to cast *all* of your cares upon Him. Look at that for a minute. He said, "all." What's left after "all?" Nothing is left. That means *everything.* Give it all to Him, He understands that you may be scared. He wants to talk to you right now. Remember, God speaks to us through His Word, and He wants to give you this Bible verse,

> Isaiah 41:10 - Don't be afraid, for I am with you, don't be discouraged, for I am your God. I will strengthen you and help you. I will uphold you with my righteous right hand.

This bible verse speaks to my heart because we have our youngest baby boy, he just turned one year a few days ago. He is just learning how to walk, and he is being introduced to new foods as well. The reason this verse reminds me of him is that he looks at us with eyes full of trust. When he is learning to take steps, he freezes in the middle of either falling or struggling to take the next step. We stand in front of him telling him, "It's ok, don't be afraid, I'll catch you."

If I am sitting down having dinner, he will want to sit and eat with me. When he is ready to try a new food he will open his little mouth, trusting that what I am going to feed him will be good. While he is developing and growing, I will hold him for that next step, ready to catch him if he falls. This is how I see that verse in God's readiness to catch us knowing that He has cleared our path and will give us the strength that we need to take that next step.

The Lord is pushing me to go deeper and for me to get personal with you, so here it goes. I am about to take you into a very personal prayer that I prayed just a few days ago. I don't mean to offend anyone by saying this, but I am not telling you this just so that you will know my business. The point behind me sharing this with you is to show you how important it is to empty ourselves to the Lord in prayer. For us to be able to go to the next level with the Lord, we can't just sit around and wait for Him to promote us. We must do our part in what we offer back to the Lord. We must put our faith into action. We do not want to rob Him of what is rightfully His, our praises, our worship, our prayers, our supplications, and our communication with God are critical to our spiritual development. Please open yourself up as you read my prayer to the Lord.

Before I begin, know a few things. Around this time, I was three months behind on my mortgage, as well as one month behind on our vehicle's repayment. My son's car broke down and was in the shop, so we loaned him one of our vehicles. The vehicle insurance was expired. I had to make payment arrangements for our electric bill, and the pink notice for disconnection for our unpaid water bill had just come in.

It was 7:30 in the morning and I was late for work. I had to take our son to school. I got in the truck full of silent emotions that were bombarding my mind, thoughts of self-condemnation were attacking my mind, but I was trying not to let my son see me upset. As I was taking him to school, he was saying his morning prayer just before I dropped him off. He said, "Bye daddy. Have a good day!" Then he leaned in to give me a goodbye kiss.

He was only eight years old at the time. As his father, I cherish these moments. As he was getting out of the vehicle, a horrible feeling came over me as if I was letting my family down. I remember feeling that they deserved better than what I have been able to offer them. But remember, the Lord has been sustaining us financially, and the Devil was trying to get me to forget how good God had always been to me. We never had extra, yet we lacked nothing. But at this moment I felt as if the walls were caving in on me, in my head I could hear the loudest silence ripping me apart. I had to pull off to the side of the road because the tears were flowing down my face and blurring my vision. I had to talk to the Lord, I just had to pray. I've never had anyone to turn to except the Lord. This is the time in my life when the Lord became my best friend, so I began to pray.

My Prayer of Faith

I pulled my truck over to the side of the highway and started to pray.

> "Lord, what's going on? I need to hear from you. I am finding myself in this place again and I don't like the way it feels. I can't seem to understand what you are doing. Why are we struggling again with our finances?

Are you not the God who freed the Israelites from Egypt? Are you not the God who saved Daniel from the hungry Lions? Lord, you are the Highest God! Lord, you are the One True Living God! Lord, I am holding on to you with everything that you created inside of me. You are my God; you are my King! Lord, I don't have to be put through a test of faith like Job, I don't answer to Satan, I don't have to prove anything to Satan. He is not whom I serve, Lord, Jesus, I serve you and only you.

You are *Jehovah Jira*, my provider. Your Word says you will make me the head and not the tail. Your Word says I will lend and not borrow. You said for me to test you with my tithes and offerings. Lord I am always pouring myself out to you. I repent of all my iniquity.

Lord, I will continue to hold on to your Word and every

promise you have written concerning me and my family. I surrender to your will for me, I give all I am to you, Lord. Father, hear my cry. Rebuke the devourer on my behalf for your name's sake." In the Name of Jesus Christ, I pray, Amen.

Deuteronomy 28:13 KJV - And the LORD shall make you the head, and not the tail; and you shall be above only, and you shall not be beneath; if that you hearken unto the commandments of the LORD your God, which I command you this day, to observe and to do them:

"Lord, your word also says that I am more than a conqueror."

Romans 8:37 - No, in all these things we are more than conquerors through him who loved us.

"Lord, your word also says that you would never leave me nor forsake me."

Deuteronomy 31:8 KJV - The LORD himself goes before you and will be with you; he will never leave you nor forsake you. Do not be afraid; do not be discouraged.

"Lord, this is your word, your promise to me as your child. My Savior, Jesus Christ's blood has allowed me to come directly to your throne and talk with you. I am covered with the blood of your Son. You sent Jesus to die for my sins, and to give me eternal life. Through Christ, I am supposed to be living life to its fullest, guided by your Holy Spirit. Lord, God in heaven, I want to see your face as Moses did. You talked to Moses as if he was talking to one of his friends. What made Moses so special that you can't talk to me the same way? I am looking for you. I want to touch you. Your Word even says we are to repent of our sins to let us reason together."

> Isaiah 1:18 KJV - Come now, and let us reason together, saith the LORD: though your sins be as scarlet, they shall be as white as snow; though they be red like crimson, they shall be as wool.

"I am reaching out to you right now, Father. Bend your ear to me and hear my cry. I am asking for more of you and less of me. I am emptying my heart and soul so that you can fill me with more of you. I can't go on like this! I know your Word says that you have no favorites, and you love us all the same. But, Lord, if there are sins in my life that are still staining my soul, I ask for forgiveness for those sins now, and I ask you through the blood of Jesus to break all the curses that I have caused and that you have permitted in my finances and my life. I am coming clean before your throne.

"Lord, I know that I don't deserve anything, but through Christ and His blood, am I not your son? I made a promise to you when I came back to you eight years ago. I have done my best to keep my mind, body, spirit, and soul clean. My lips have not tasted alcohol, nor have I smoked anything since the day I made that promise. Lord, don't my faithfulness, obedience, and dedication to you count for something? You said to come and let us reason together. I'm waiting, Lord! While I wait, I will be faithful and patient. I just need to know that you are still with me. Lord, there are filthy preachers out there who are not loyal to you. They are full of lust and wickedness, using your name for profit and self-promotion. Here we are silently faithfully waiting to hear from you as we get deeper and deeper in debt.

"Father God, hear me. Lord, I am calling out to you. Fill me with a double portion of your Holy Spirit. Fill me with your grace and favor. Grant me wisdom to discern that which is from you and that which isn't. I need you to step in for me.

"As you sit on your high and mighty throne, look down on me. I need you to break through for me and the family you have given me. I will be trusting you, Lord. I will be waiting and listening for your voice. I have done what you have told me to do with all my heart. Your turn, In Jesus's name I pray, Amen."

Friend, isn't it time for you to cast all your cares on Him? He cares for you. Can you relate to my prayer? Have you ever felt this way? Today is your day, it's your turn to live in His fulness and favor. How much do you love Him? Talk to Him and give Him all you've got. He is waiting to hear from you right now. Cast all your cares on Him for He cares so much for you.

I am reminded of when God provided *manna* for His people. Remember when He brought His people out of Egypt? He provided the bread of heaven for them to eat daily. They were to eat as much as they wanted and not store any of it for tomorrow. If they were to store some for the next day, it would rot and waste. Jesus Christ is the Bread from heaven that we need, His Grace is sufficient to meet our every need. Every day is a fresh anointing from the Lord. We don't have to worry about it running out, there is an endless supply. There is enough for the whole world.

Exodus 16:13-20 KJV

> 13) That evening quail came and covered the camp, and in the morning, there was a layer of dew around the camp.
>
> 14) When the dew was gone, thin flakes like frost on the ground appeared on the desert floor.
>
> 15) When the Israelites saw it, they said to each other, "What is it?" For they did not know what it was.
>
> Moses said to them, "It is the bread the Lord has given you to eat.
>
> 16) This is what the Lord has commanded: 'Everyone is to gather as much as they need. Take an omer for each person you have in your tent.'
>
> 17) The Israelites did as they were told; some gathered much, some little.
>
> 18) And when they measured it by the omer, the one who gathered much did not have too much, and the one who gathered little did not have too little. Everyone had gathered just as much as they needed.
>
> 19) Then Moses said to them, "No one is to keep any of it until morning."
>
> 20) However, some of them paid no attention to Moses; they kept part of it until morning, but it was full of maggots and began to smell. So, Moses was angry with them.

Friend, come to Jesus exactly the way you are at this moment. You don't have to fix your condition or situation first. Bring all your troubles and fears and find your rest. Take what the Lord is offering you today. There is plenty of God's grace for you and your loved ones. It is time for you and your loved ones to experience the power of God. There is so much more that awaits you through Jesus Christ. The Lord says to cast all your cares on Him for He cares for you. Friend, if you follow Jesus, everything will be okay. You are going to get through the storm, and you will come out victorious on the other side. Give the Lord your worries and your fears. He's waiting for you right now.

LEANDRO OLIVAREZ

Chapter 10

Time to Live

I have often wondered if I was the only person on earth who always felt like I was waiting for my life to start. I would often say things like, "When the time is right, I will do this or that." I would think things like, "One day I will go here or there," as if I was waiting for the proper time, or someone's approval, or a sign from God. Then one day I realized that I was already in my early thirties. I had been living with the mentality that I was waiting for my life to start but the reality was that my life was passing me by, slipping right through my fingers. I could not understand what was holding me back from succeeding in life. When, I wondered, would I see some of my dreams come true?

It's time to accept the reality of where you are in life right now and to do a self-assessment so that you can release yourself from things that you are holding on. Those things are doing you more damage than good. It's time for you to heal and bury the hurt and disappointments of the past. This way, you can move forward and start living. Either way, the clock is ticking and each day that passes is a day that we are closer to eternity.

In my case, I was sitting around waiting for things to happen as if my dreams were supposed to fall out of the sky and land in my lap or something. What in the world was I thinking? It's almost as if there was an invisible wall separating my mind from the reality of true happiness and purpose. One day, I thought, "Where has my life gone?" I felt as if I was twenty-one years old just last year. But the harsh reality was that I was twenty years old over ten years ago. Oh my gosh! What do I do now? At a young age, I concluded, we all think we are special because we grow up being told by our mothers that we are special. I felt I was created to be a world changer. There is some truth to that by the way. We are each special in our own way. But the world around you will never know how special you are if you don't start living and interacting with people, get out there, and share your faith with someone. Tell someone how good God has been to you.

It wasn't until around the age of about twenty-eight that my eyes were opened, and I knew that I had to start living, but how? I didn't know how to do anything other than chase after a fantasy life of music, lies, drugs, and recognition. Looking back at my younger years, I realize that I was rejected by people and so-called friends. I had rejection issues but didn't realize it. I was an angry, negative person, afraid to be rejected, and I dealt with self-rejection. I never knew how to be happy. I didn't want to be fake. I made many bad choices for the sake of "being accepted." The Lord recently showed me the reason I could never be happy. Even though my life was great, inside I just couldn't figure out the source of my problem until the Lord showed me that an evil spirit of "discontent" that was keeping my mind bound. I had to cast it out and break its demonic stronghold over the patterns of my mind. This demon was keeping me from knowing that I was created with a greater purpose for my life. That was the key right there, "living with purpose."

I can't help but wonder how many of us can step out of our life boxes and look inside and be brutally honest with ourselves to see our way of day-to-day life. Are you honestly able to say that you have been living your life with a life-changing purpose? I hope you can, but for me, I was so lost I never fit in anywhere or with anyone. I was never a loner, but even surrounded by a group of people, I would feel very alone.

I am being transparent not so you would read my story and think, "Wow, that's a good story." Instead, I hope you will take my experience, along with my mistakes, and compare my life to yours to help guide you in the right direction, to begin living your life with purpose. For me, it wasn't until I met the woman who would later be my wife. If you've read my first book, *A New Life Is Expecting You*, you know that she had an awesome six-year-old boy whose father had never been around.

One day I was at my soon-to-be wife's apartment and her little boy, Jacob, had his bags packed to go stay the weekend with his father. He had his little backpack on the floor by the back door, where he was sitting at the dining room table looking out of the window waiting for his father to show up and take him away for the weekend. Oh, my Lord, little Jacob would silently cry his heart out because his father wouldn't show up. So, without anyone knowing, I would go into the restroom where I could be alone, and I would cry for him because his crying would break my heart. Then, I would take a few minutes to compose myself, wash my face, and then go into his room, put my arm around him to comfort him.

I didn't see it at the time but looking back now, the Lord was giving me purpose to be the man that God intended me to be for this little boy. He needed a daddy, and I needed a son. I felt something deep inside me telling me that if I wasn't going to change my life and be the man that this woman and this little boy needed, then what I needed to do was leave because they had seen enough heartache and disappointment. This for me was the first sign of real purpose in my life.

I didn't recognize it at the time, but now as the years have passed, God directing our lives, I see how God gave me what I needed through them and gave them what they needed through me. God himself had to be the foundation of this new relationship that was forming. Since then, he has been my son. I legally adopted him. He is now twenty-six years old bearing my last name and has become an amazing God-fearing man. He is my son, the oldest of four, my firstborn. My wife and I have since had three more beautiful children together. God is too good to us when we don't deserve it. But if you are hungry for God, and if you find yourself longing for more out of life, My Lord Jesus Christ will come through for you.

The blessings from God will never stop coming if you are obedient to the Lord, He will always take care of you. About four years ago my father, who also happens to be my senior pastor, called my wife and me over to their house. I had been preaching for about four years and had helped them with prayer requests and prayer calls. They sat us down and my father asked if I would be his Associate Pastor. I thought, "Wow!" My wife and I were both brought to tears. After praying about for about a week, I called them and let them know that I accepted this great honor to serve.

Friend, you too have a purpose. Have you made the time to slow life down a little so that you may be able to identify that God has so much more for you and your family? Here is the best part, you not only have a purpose, but you have a greater purpose. Know that God has heard your every prayer, and that God is on the move and answering the prayers of His people. It is time for you to see that you are loved so much that God sent His only son to die for our sins and God sent Jesus to be our ultimate blood sacrifice. That is why Jesus Christ is the only one who can wash our sins away. Jesus Christ is the one who hung on that cross so that we could be forgiven of all our sins, trespasses, transgressions, and our iniquity.

Please remember that God is a Spirit. The way He walks with us and talks to us is through His Holy Spirit. That means we must get to a place in our Christian walk where we start to recognize the difference between our flesh and the Spirit. We need to be able to recognize when God is coming through for us. We need to develop an effective prayer life and spiritually apply the blood of Jesus Christ over ourselves and our homes and loved ones. The blood of Jesus is the robe of righteousness. Be sure to put it on daily, and don't miss this word to you from the Lord: One of the biggest reasons we miss when God has answered our prayer is that we seem to think He will answer us the way that we want Him to. Remember that God told us His ways are not our ways, and His thoughts are not our thoughts. We must develop our relationship with the Lord through His Holy Spirit.

In the same manner that we find ourselves longing for more out of life, the Lord also longs to hear from us, and desires a relationship with us as well. Please don't miss this. I am not just giving you positive words, the Lord told me to tell you that He loves you. We end up missing our blessing or a word from the Lord if we constantly look in the wrong direction. We want God to answer us our way, and we rarely pray, "Lord, your will be done."

It is very common among believers to say, "Please agree with me that my plan works out." But wait a minute. We must remember that God does things in His own way. He says in his Word, "that His ways are not our ways, and our ways are not His ways."

<u>Isaiah 55:8-12 KJV</u>

> 8) For my thoughts are not your thoughts, neither are your ways my ways, saith the Lord.
>
> 9) For as the heavens are higher than the earth, so are my ways higher than your ways, and my thoughts than your thoughts.
>
> 10) For as the rain cometh down, and the snow from heaven, and returneth not thither, but watereth the earth, and maketh it brings forth and bud, that it may give seed to the sower, and bread to the eater:
>
> 11) So shall my word be that goeth forth out of my mouth: it shall not return unto me void, but it shall accomplish that which I please,

and it shall prosper in the thing whereto I sent it.

12) For ye shall go out with joy and be led forth with peace: the mountains and the hills shall break forth before you into singing, and all the trees of the field shall clap their hands.

The Lord wants to give you His peace, He wants you to be joyful. It is a good thing for you to be a joyful person, to live in expectation. There is a big difference between happiness and joyfulness. I often refer to happiness as temporary because it is circumstantial. We become bipolar holy rollers instead of living joyfully every day in expectation for God to fulfill His promises and His will for our lives. Let the power of God manifest in your life, don't get in your own way.

I am excited to know that the Lord's love is rushing into your life and heart like a flood of anointed waters. His word also says that "In the last days, He will pour out His Spirit on all flesh." That means anyone who will allow God to do what He wants to do in their lives. I encourage you today to start to investigate God's Word. Don't rush through it. Set a goal to read His Word slowly, asking Him to give you spiritual understanding.

Ask the Lord, to anoint you, to baptize you in the baptism of the Holy Spirit. He will open your understanding and you will be able to see things in the spirit realm and then be able to understand things that you have never understood before. This will be the real encounter with Jesus Christ and a wholesome feeling of clarity and gratification will come into your spirit life.

This is the actual Holy Spirit of God who will manifest in you as well as through you if you come to Jesus Christ with all your heart with no motive other than you know that you are a sinner and that you know that you are in need for God in your life. It is at this stage that if your heart is in the right place, your inner motives are lined up with God's will, then brace yourself. God is about to begin to reveal Himself to you in ways that you could never imagine.

If you find yourself in this place where you feel ready for a change, then I am overjoyed for you because you are about to start living the very best part of your life. God has already planted a seed inside of you of greater purpose. But what do you have to do with a seed? Make sure that it's in good soil (your heart), then water it. Give that seed the light it needs. Study God's Word and get to know Him. The light your seed needs is Jesus. The water your seed needs is the Holy Spirit. When you are in a relationship with a person, there must be communication for that relationship to be effective. Well, then how can we say that we have a relationship with God the Father through Jesus Christ if we don't even know what His Word says? We can't! Look at it this way. It will help put the Word of God (The Holy Bible) into perspective.

Suppose I recorded a video for my children. Currently, my children are little but if I were to die before they grew up, this video that I would record for them would be of me giving them advice and instructions for life, what to do and what not to do. I would instruct them according to what worked and what didn't work for me and their mother.

In the video, there would be relationship advice, advice on how to buy a vehicle, what to do and what not to do. In case I have not mentioned it before, I was a car salesman for a few years, so here is what I would tell them when they are ready to go and buy a vehicle.

I would say,

> "Kids remember, this is rule number one. When you purchase a vehicle, never allow the salesman to know exactly how much money you have in your pocket, always tell him that you have half of what you do have because you must allow yourself room for taxes, title

fees, and license fees. If you are trading in a vehicle, they will point out every fault of your vehicle, faded paint, tire condition, racket windshield, etc. They will try to diminish the value of your trade, so you do the same to their vehicle if you are buying a pre-owned vehicle. Stick to the dollar amount that you want for your car as a trade. They will make a deal work, but remember, don't ever run a credit report, or sign a single sheet of paper until you are ready to buy because they will drop your name in a Credit Union bank pond of over fifteen to twenty banks that will be looking at your credit report and your credit score will take a hit for each one! Don't allow this to happen.

"Also, the way your mom and I bought our first house, we put at least five thousand dollars in the bank for three months then we applied for a specific loan, and we were approved for our first home."

The examples would continue with advice for each one. I would also provide spiritual direction, relationship advice, and so forth. Friend, don't you think this would be very beneficial to my children? In a way, I would always be with them even when I am gone and with the Lord. Well, my friend, this is exactly what the Holy Bible (the Word of God) is for us. It is God's living Word and a guide for His children, That's us.

Friend, it's not too late to live in the full potential God intends for you to live. Many of the men in the Bible were old men, some of them in their eighties if not older. And when I speak of "blessings and living to your full potential" I am not speaking of just financial goals. Some people when they think of God blessing them automatically assume that means money. Money has nothing to do with you starting to live a full, happy, and fulfilled life in Christ. It can be as simple as knowing exactly what you have and respecting, honoring, cherishing, understanding, and dedicating yourself to what or who you have. God can choose to bless you any way He wants to, and He will bless you according to your faith and obedience to Him.

For some it may be money, and for others it may be good health, happiness, respect, or even something as simple as just wanting to be loved. Don't wait for your life to begin. Friend, your spouse and children should already know how much you love them, build them up and never put them down. Sometimes people need to slow down and realize that their life has already begun.

In the Bible, there is a story of a man named Elisha and his servant. I love this story. You will see how God tells His people to brace themselves because He was about to do something huge, their lives were all about to change. Here is the story of how this happened.

2 KINGS 6:8-17 KJV

> 8) Now the king of Aram was at war with Israel. After conferring with his officers, he said, "I will set up my camp in such and such a place."
>
> 9) The man of God sent word to the king of Israel: "Beware of passing that place, because the Arameans are going down there."
>
> 10) So the king of Israel checked on the place indicated by the man of God. Time and again Elisha warned the king, so that he was on his guard in such places.
>
> 11) This enraged the king of Aram. He summoned his officers and demanded of them, "tell me! Which of us is on the side of the king of Israel?"
>
> 12) "None of us, my lord the king," said one of his officers, "but Elisha, the prophet who is in Israel, tells the king of Israel the very

words you speak in your bedroom."

13) "Go, find out where he is," the king ordered, "so I can send men and capture him." The report came back: "He is in Dothan."

14) Then he sent horses and chariots and a strong force there. They went by night and surrounded the city.

15) When the servant of the man of God got up and went out early the next morning, an army with horses and chariots had surrounded the city. "Oh no, my lord! What shall we do?" the servant asked.

16 "Don't be afraid," the prophet answered. "Those who are with us are more than those who are with them."

17) And Elisha prayed, "Open his eyes, Lord, so that he may see." Then the Lord opened the servant's eyes, and he looked and saw the hills full of horses and chariots of fire all around Elisha.

Let's take a closer look at this. There are two individuals. One is a firm believer in God and the other is his servant. I am pretty sure the servant was just a normal guy like you and me. What I mean by, "a normal guy like us" is that he says he believes in God and God's power but when he is faced with difficulty, fear takes him over. He didn't know what to do, he was scared because he was surrounded by the enemy, he was about to be attacked. How many times do we find ourselves in that same kind of mindset? After being God's child and being taught about spiritual warfare, we should already know about the "Full Amor of God," "Binding and Loosing," and "Our Authority In Jesus Christ," as well as understanding what Jesus did on the cross and what it means for us.

The other guy (Elisha) understood the power of God. He understood God's love because he had a daily relationship with God. Elisha was not perfect, but he was used by God in mighty ways because he believed and through his obedience, he trusted God. So now let's take a life-changing moment to step back. Examine your spiritual life right now and compare these two different people, one man is afraid of the unknown and the other is confident in who his God is. Now stop! Ask yourself this one question, taking the two different levels of belief from these two men. Which one are you most like?

This is where your spiritual breakthrough is! It's right in front of you. I hope that you can see the difference between the two and recognize how there is a new level waiting for you. But it is up to you to believe in your God, and to know your God on a personal level. Understand, no matter how bad or how lonely you may feel, as a child of the Most High God, you have thousands of angels surrounding you on chariots of fire waiting to defend you. Those that are for you will always outnumber and are stronger than those that are against you.

Now, my friend, knowing how valuable you truly are to the Lord, how much more confidently will you face tomorrow? It is time to start living the way God intended for you to live. You are not a victim of circumstance! You are more than a conqueror through Christ, and you are under His grace, mercy, love, protection, and power. Under the direct guidance of the Holy Spirit Himself. Sometimes, friend, all you must do is stand in your place and the Lord will dust you off. Prepare yourself. From this day forward you will start to live a life of greater purpose through Jesus Christ. Welcome to the first day of your new life.

> 2 Corinthians 5:17 KJV - Therefore, if any man is in Christ, he is a new creature: old things are passed away; behold, all things become new.

The fresh new start that you have been looking for is now within reach, allow Christ to wash your sins away and become the person that you have always desired to be. With no guilt and no self-condemnation, it's your move. Just talk to the Lord, I will help you right now. Just pray this with all your heart to the Lord.

> Lord Jesus, I know that I am a sinner. I believe that you are the son of God as well as God the son. I ask you now to please forgive me of all my sins, transgressions, trespasses, and the iniquity in my bloodline. Lord, come into my heart and be my Lord and my Savior. I receive you by faith. I believe that from this moment on I am forgiven, I am Saved, Delivered, and Healed according to your word. In Jesus's name, I pray.
>
> Amen…

Matthew 6:33 KJV - But seek ye first the kingdom of God, and his righteousness; and all these things shall be added unto you.

Congratulations! You are about to embark on the journey of your life. The Lord will soon introduce you to the real person He created you to be. Get yourself mentally ready for your new Life in Christ. It's time to live.

Chapter 11

General of War

A few days ago, I was reading in the Bible where Joshua was anointed by God to lead His people. And after a close examination of the scriptures, we come to see that Joshua is a type of Christ Jesus. I was instantly drawn into the Holy Scriptures, and I just couldn't get enough. This is what I want to share with you today. But first, know that as a believer in Christ Jesus, everything that I am about to share with you is about you. Yes, you. Sometimes we go through seasons in our lives where we just can't see a glimpse of hope, and we feel very discouraged about the direction that life has been taking us. This is the reason why I believe that God wants me to share this Biblical story with you, and we will be breaking it down as we go through it.

As I mentioned before, this is about the biblical warrior named Joshua. In Hebrew, his name is "Yehoshua," meaning Yahweh is deliverance. I find that so fascinating because the name Jesus is "Yeshua," meaning "to rescue to deliver." I absolutely love this, and as we see in Scriptures, Joshua became the leader God chose to lead the Israelite tribes after the death of Moses, and Joshua conquered Canaan and distributed its lands to the twelve.

There is no doubt about it, Joshua is a man of war, and he will go wherever God tells him to go. Here is why this is so important for the Lord's church today. From Joshua, we learn that we need to get dressed for battle in the full armor of God every day and go out and possess what God has promised to His people. God's blessings aren't just going to fall out of the sky onto our lap. We must get up and move forward in His name and fight for our blessings. Sometimes those blessings come in the form of peace of mind, salvation, healing, and restoration. One must realize that when you are in a battle, you can't just stop moving. You are on the front lines of the spiritual battle fighting for your health, fighting for your sanity, and fighting for your family.

Once the battle is over, the warrior comes home to his family in victory, to rest and recoup and enjoy the life that he fought for but must never get too comfortable because the Bible tells us that the Devil prowls around like a roaring lion seeking whom he may devour. To you, that means, to stay ready because another battle will be coming soon. Like Joshua, when it comes to the enemy, we must approach the battlefield of the mind and fight him in the name of our Lord Jesus Christ. We must violently strip the enemy of all legal rights that he has robbed from us and that we have forfeited to him through our season of rebellion against God. It's time for you and your loved ones to be restored, in the name of Jesus Christ. Let's dive into what God wants to show you today.

Joshua 10: KJV

> 1) Now it came to pass, when Adonizedec king of Jerusalem had heard how Joshua had taken Ai, and had utterly destroyed it; as he had done to Jericho and her king, so he had done to Ai and her king; and how the inhabitants of Gibeon had made peace with Israel, and were among them.

We see in this verse that the king of Jerusalem is in fear that Joshua will attack them, and the king is about to call for his alliance kings to come and help them fight. He knows of Joshua's reputation in war, and he dreads having to face Joshua and his army. This is the kind of spiritual reputation I would love to have. Wouldn't you love to know you have a good reputation of prayer, fasting, and worship, that demons had to think lon and hard before attacking you because of your reputation with the Holy Spirit? Yes, that is where we are going with this.

> 2) That they feared greatly, because Gibeon was a great city, as one of the royal cities, and because it was greater than Ai, and all the men thereof were mighty.

The name of this king is Adoni-Zedec. I find it strange that God's name Adoni is in this man's name. Adoni in Hebrew is a name for God, and the name Zedec is used more as a suffix, to describe all of Jerusalem's kings, which gives us the meaning of Zedec as "righteous." The important thing that to see is that depending on your spiritual rank, even the enemy will have to call for backup in his fight against you, but notice that the enemy will just call one principality and he will come armed with several because that Devil's mission is to take you out. Position yourself in Christ to make those demons regret coming after you, and they will be demoted and humiliated in their kingdom.

Wouldn't it be awesome for a demon to have to go back to his superior and report that they failed in their mission because they are covered in the blood of Jesus Christ of Nazareth? They would be openly disgraced. But that would mean getting yourself ready in the Lord because their reinforcements will be next to come against you. Yes, we know in Christ you have victory if you fight! Because God doesn't bless the lazy.

> 3) Wherefore Adonizedec king of Jerusalem, sent unto Hoham king of Hebron, and unto Piram king of Jarmuth, and unto Japhia king of Lachish, and unto Debir king of Eglon, saying,
>
> 4) Come up unto me, and help me, that we may smite Gibeon: for it hath made peace with Joshua and with the children of Israel.

When you look carefully at this verse, you will notice that when you make peace with "Yeshua Jesus" (Josh-u-ah) the Lord, the Lord's enemies will come out of the woodwork. If the enemy sees Jesus in you, the enemy will have to call for backup. We are looking at a total of five kings, which is five different armies. If the enemy hates us that bad, then why should we spare these demons and why should we allow these Devils to attack our homes and our families. The enemy takes this war way more seriously than the church. Why doesn't the church fight back in the power of the Holy Spirit? These enemies need to be threatened by you. They must see Jesus in you.

> 5) Therefore, the five kings of the Amorites, the king of Jerusalem, the king of Hebron, the king of Jarmuth, the king of Lachish, the king of Eglon, gathered themselves together, and went up, they and all their hosts, and encamped before Gibeon, and made war against it.
>
> 6) And the men of Gibeon sent unto Joshua to the camp to Gilgal, saying, Slack not thy hand from thy servants; come up to us quickly, and save us, and help us: for all the kings of the Amorites that dwell in the mountains are gathered against us.

We believers in Jesus Christ must turn to our Lord, our heavenly Joshua, for every battle we face in this life. The Bible tells us that they that call on the name of the Lord, shall be saved. We must hold on to and treasure God's Word because the Word became flesh and made His dwelling among us, that is Christ Jesus. Remember that our Lord Jesus has never lost a battle.

> 7) So, Joshua ascended from Gilgal, he, and all the people of war with him, and all the mighty men of valor.
>
> 8) And the Lord said unto Joshua, fear them not: for I have

> delivered them into thine hand; there shall not a man of them stand before thee. 9) Joshua therefore came unto them suddenly and went up from Gilgal all night.

It is so awesome how this should be the foundation for every believer, the absolute assurance that God Himself is with us, the courage to walk in the name of the Lord with no fear in sight, that demon of fear should remember when you cast him out of your mind and should know better than to come near your bloodline again.

God told Joshua, "I have delivered the enemy into your hands." Notice God did not say "I *will deliver*." He said, "I *have delivered*," which means because of your close relationship with the Father, the Son, and the Holy Spirit, the Lord will move on your behalf before you even arrive at the battlefield. Joshua sets an Ambush on the enemy.

Position yourself to ambush the enemy that is surrounding your home, the enemy that is surrounding your loved ones. The way you can do that is through prayer, fasting, worshiping, and praising the Lord. Praying in the Spirit. Remember that there is no interpretation available for the prayer language of tongues. I am not talking about the divers gift of tongues. I am referring to the prayer language. This is an extremely powerful weapon because neither the Devil nor his demons understand this prayer language. Only the Father, Son, and Holy Spirit understand this language and that sends the enemy's camp into utter chaos.

The Bible says that we are seated with Christ in the heavenly realm at the right hand of the Father. One should never try to fight the enemy on his grounds or his terms, the battlefield being the mind. The Devil knows that if he conquers your mind, then he can claim your territory. Ambush the enemy not from the ground, not from the first heaven, which is our sky, nor the second heaven, which is where our moon, sun, and stars are located. We must ambush from our position from the third heaven from where we are seated with Christ in the Heavenly realm. Hit him, and hit him hard with the Word of God. Learn the scriptures and fight for God's promises for yourself and your family.

> 10) And the Lord discomfited them before Israel, and slew them with a great slaughter at Gibeon, and chased them along the way that goeth up to Bethhoron, and smote them to Azekah, and unto Makkedah.

The Lord will embarrass His enemies. I love how the enemy was chased down. The distance between these locations is about a twenty-five-mile stretch. We should treat our spiritual enemy as "an enemy." Remind yourself that the Devil is out to destroy you and your children and your children's children. I can't stress this enough to be a true representative of the Lord. We must give what we have freely received from the Lord, "His love."

Friend, move forward in His love. In His love you will find the power and the strength to carry on. When those times of weakness and discouragement come, hold on to the Lord with everything you have, and cast down those strongholds in the name of Jesus Christ. Let your faith remain strong. Show your faith in the Lord, and He will certainly sustain you and walk with you everywhere you go. Never give up to the enemy just give in to Jesus Christ.

Chapter 12

Instructions for Battle

As I write this, we are in June of 2022, and I am just thinking about how good God has been to me and my family. Reflecting on this past year, I can see how the Lord has brought us through some major storms. Just last February I found myself fighting for my life. I came down with a case of COVID-19. This was a tough battle, but like everything else I go through I have learned to turn my attention toward the spiritual reality rather than focus on the physical situation.

One day while I was at work, I started to feel very weak, so I pushed myself to get through the workday, to come home to just collapse on the floor of my living room. I am going to change some names of people in this story so no one will feel like I am blaming them. I wouldn't do something like that. A few days before me feeling sick, our church had just finished a food drive on a Saturday afternoon, and I was the last person there and was getting ready to leave the Church when a brother in Christ showed up moments before I was about to lock the door.

Brother Mark pulled up and said, "Hey Pastor! Do you have any food left over?" As he got out of his vehicle and walked toward me to greet me.

I replied, "Brother Mark, it is good to see you, I haven't seen you in a while." He greeted me with a handshake and a hug. I said, "How is Sister Amy (his wife)"?

He said, "Oh pastor, she is at home dealing with COVID."

I said, "She's what? Are you telling me that she has COVID?"

He said, "Yes and I am running a fever, I can't stop sweating, I feel very hot!"

I said, "Brother, you should have stayed in your car. I would have handed the food to you through the open window. Brother, why did you come to me and hug me? You know I have a family at home."

He said, "I'm sorry pastor, but I am headed to my son's house to help him work on his car."

I was upset that someone would be so inconsiderate of others. I prayed for the both of us right away, handed him several bags of food, and sent him on his way.

The next morning, I was at the pulpit preaching, feeling very thirsty, with a slight headache. I didn't get close to anyone, but I did announce to the church to keep their distance from me because I wasn't feeling well so the whole church stretched their hands toward me and prayed for me. There is a part of our service after the preaching when I invite people to come up for prayer, but this time I explained that I wasn't going to do that this day. I would pray for everyone from a distance and from the pulpit where I was standing.

Now comes Monday morning, the third day after my encounter with Brother Mark. I awoke with a slight fever, feeling achy all over and very dehydrated. I started to pray and ask God for His divine protection over myself and my family. At home, I have my three young children and my wife. Our oldest son lives on his own. I was worried about them.

I took myself to the emergency room, and they asked me, "Why are we seeing you today?" I said, "I think I am just dehydrated because I can't shake this headache." So, the nurse stuck my hand to prepare me for an IV, but never actually hooked me up to the IV. After about half an hour the nurse came back into the room and said to me, "Sir, we will be admitting you to the COVID floor." I said, "No you're not! You haven't even checked me yet. You still haven't given me the IV, and I haven't even seen the doctor."

She said, "Sir, we will be taking you up soon."

This didn't feel right to me. I heard the voice of the Holy Spirit say to me, "Leave now. This is not where you belong right now. The Devil is making a move against you."

I immediately said to the nurse, "Disconnect me please." She said, "No sir, I know that you have COVID. We must admit you!" Her demeanor changed. She was becoming aggressive with her words. I heard the voice of the Holy Spirit again say, "Go now!" So, I said, "If you do not disconnect me, I will disconnect myself." She said, "Well sir, I shouldn't let you leave but I can't force you to stay, and we will need to fill out some voluntary discharge papers for you to sign." I said, "Fine, get what you need to get, or I will just walk out."

The Holy Spirit had been revealing that the enemy had been plotting against me for a while. Looking back now, about two weeks before all of this, the Lord awoke me from a dream about two o'clock in the morning. In the dream, the Holy Spirit or an angel took me to a demonic council meeting. He took me to a dark room like you would see in an old-school mafia movie. The room was filled with smoke, and it was as if I was looking in through a glass window, but I wasn't, I was actually in the room.

There were three tall slim disfigured demons standing in front of me conversing with three more that were sitting at a round table. I could hear what they were saying. I found myself getting nervous. The angel that was with me told me, "Do not be afraid. They cannot see us, and they cannot hear us. They are planning your destruction, and they are planning the attack against you." It was as if the angel and I were invisible, and they were in 3D. The Angel said to me, "Be alert, but do not fear. The Lord is with you."

This reminded me of when David spoke of the council of the wicked planning against him.

> Psalm 64:2 KJV - Hide me from the secret counsel of the wicked, from the insurrection of the workers of iniquity:

So, here we are two weeks later getting ready to leave the emergency room. As I was walking out of the ER around one o'clock in the morning, I was thanking the Lord for my release. I felt at peace but at the same time, the Holy Spirit revealed to me that I was under attack. This was His warning to me. Now is the time for me to submit to my Lord and ask Him for instruction for this battle. This attack is spiritual. As a believer in Christ Jesus, we must get dressed every day in the full armor of God, to be able to resist the schemes of the Devil and extinguish his fiery arrows.

Ephesians 6:10-18 KJV

> 10) Finally, my brethren, be strong in the Lord, and the power of his might.
>
> 11) Put on the whole armor of God, that ye may be able to stand against the wiles of the Devil.
>
> 12) For we wrestle not against flesh and blood, but against principalities, against powers, against the rulers of the darkness of this world, against spiritual wickedness in high places.
>
> 13) Wherefore take unto you the whole armor of God, that ye may be able to withstand in the evil day, and having done all, to stand.
>
> 14) Stand therefore, having your loins girt about with truth, and having on the breastplate of righteousness.

> 15) And your feet shod with the preparation of the gospel of peace.
>
> 16) Above all, taking the shield of faith, wherewith ye shall be able to quench all the fiery darts of the wicked.
>
> 17) And take the helmet of salvation, and the sword of the Spirit, which is the word of God:
>
> 18) Praying always with all prayer and supplication in the Spirit and watching thereunto with all perseverance and supplication for all saints.

The fight was on! I knew what I was facing. This was clearly a spiritual battle, a battle for life. It was go time! I went into prayer. It took two days to get an appointment with my doctor, and even then, it was an appointment through Zoom. I was instructed to go to the parking lot of his office to be swabbed for COVID, so I went and the next day I was informed that I was positive for COVID-19. By this time, I had already been sick for a week, and now my wife and daughter were also COVID-positive. This was going to be the fight of my life.

As the days passed, I was getting physically worse. I could barely breathe. My wife and daughter didn't get it as bad as I did, but it was still a serious situation. My oxygen level was in the low eighties. I couldn't walk ten steps without my heart and breath racing. I would cough uncontrollably. We didn't eat for days at a time, and it got to the point where we could only eat certain fruit like berries and melons. I could hardly walk, breathe, and I had to sleep on my stomach or my side. I couldn't bathe myself for days because I didn't have the strength to walk the fifteen steps into our restroom and stand in the shower without gasping for air while under a cough attack. I prayed to the Lord, "Father God, you said that you would not allow the diseases of this world to destroy your people. Lord, come to our rescue and save us. I cancel the enemy's assignment of death and infirmity in the name of Jesus Christ. Lord, I stand firm on your Word, and hold you to your promise.

> Deuteronomy 7:15 KJV - And the LORD will take away from thee all sickness and will put none of the evil diseases of Egypt, which thou knowest, upon thee; but will lay them upon all of them that hate thee.

The Devil showed up

One night it got so bad. I had just finished praying. Understand, I felt as if my life was slipping away. I was having so much trouble breathing. I thanked the Lord that my sister Shawni was bringing us food. My two younger boys had to be secluded in their bedroom and my daughter in her room. It felt as if this was the end of me. My daughter and my wife were doing better than I was. I can remember that night around three o'clock in the morning my room getting so cold. I reached over to hold my wife's hand, and I just started to cry, gasping for air I said, "Babe, thank you for everything, I love you and the kids with all my heart. Please forgive me if I have ever hurt you. I have never in my life ever meant to hurt you. Please if I have, I'm sorry." She said, "Stop talking like that. The Lord is with us. I love you too."

I was at the point where fear was setting in because I was afraid to fall asleep and not wake up. The bedroom was so cold that I was shivering under the sheets. My wife had fallen asleep. I felt a very dark presence enter the room, and I turned over to lie on my side and to my surprise, this being that looked filthy was sitting right beside me. It was looking at me as if it was examining me. The best way I can describe him is as if his body was not human. His skin was like the faded scales of a fish or a snake, and didn't have human legs or hands, but it was as if his legs were crossed, and his hands were on what would be his knees but didn't have actual knees or actual hands. His fingers were long, and I only saw three, I didn't see his body, but it was as if his body was hidden in the darkness of the room.

I could barely speak because of the lack of oxygen, but something came over me and the fear left me. I knew this was the Devil in physical form. I looked at him as if I knew exactly who he was, without hesitation, I said to him, "Who are you?" He was still staring at me and with a smooth seductive, feminine yet masculine voice said to me, "You know who I am Le-an-dro," as he said my name very slowly. I then said to him, "What are you doing here?" He said to me, with a slithering sarcastic response, "You know what I am doing here." Something came over me, a strength that I did not have, with a confidence that I cannot explain, I said these words, "Look here Devil, this is how it is, as for me and my house we will serve the Lord Jesus Christ, and you have two seconds to leave my home and take this sickness with you before I call upon the Holy Spirit to drag you out of here kicking and screaming." His demeanor changed as if he was disturbed. He paused for a few seconds and said, "Fine!" Then he left the room.

I reached over, grabbed my phone, and turned on some worship music. I went into worship thanking the Lord for coming to my rescue, as I started praying and worshipping the Lord, I remember the presence of God filling my room and my home at four o'clock in the morning as I started singing along with the song, "Above all wisdom and all the ways of man you were here before the world began." I just remember that with all my heart I was so grateful. By this time, we had been sick for two and a half weeks. Looking back now, I had a choice to submit to the fear, or submit to the Lord. If I had submitted to fear, I would have failed the test and the enemy would have won. But God's Word tells us to submit to God and resist the Devil and he will flee.

> James 4:7 KJV - Submit yourselves therefore to God. Resist the Devil, and he will flee from you.

I fell asleep in the presence of God as if the Lord was holding me in His arms. It was the very next day that we all started to feel much better, and we started to recover. The Lord immediately started the recovery process in all three of us. We must trust in the Lord; the Church must develop a deep relationship with the Holy Spirit and learn to hear His voice. When you learn to recognize the voice of the Holy Spirit, you will also learn to identify your battle and learn to pick your spiritual fight. Some battles belong to you and some battles belong to the Lord. However, either way, the Lord will always be with you. Remember the teacher is never far away when the test is underway. The power of God is inside each of us. Trust Him, with childlike faith. The Lord truly loves us, and He walks with us. His Word says that He will never leave us nor forsake us.

> Joshua 1:5 KJV - "There shall not any man be able to stand before thee all the days of thy life: as I was with Moses, so I will be with thee: I will not fail thee, nor forsake thee."

Paralyzed Snakes

The most recent attack came a couple of months ago. The Lord visited me in a dream, and in this dream, I was at an old house, which looked familiar to me, but it wasn't my house. I don't know whom this house belonged to. The dream went like this. I was walking up to this house and had to open the gate to get in. As I crossed through the gate and was walking up to the house, it was as if I was given a vision from above the house as if something lifted me above the house.

I could hear the voices of children in the backyard. Now I was able to see the children pointing to a large poisonous snake in striking position near the house, but I couldn't get to them because of a separate fence surrounding the back part of the house. I could not even go through the house because it was locked. As I was brought back down to ground level, I noticed that there was a tunnel that ran from the side of the house to the backyard to the spot where the children were standing and pointing to that large snake.

I decided to crawl through this pitch-black tunnel. I had this sense of urgency to get to the children to kill that snake before it bit someone. I was crawling through and as I was about to come through, someone said, "Be careful! The snake is facing you and ready to strike." I said, "Lord Jesus, cover me with your blood. Give me wisdom to trap and kill this snake in the name of Jesus. Amen." I peeked my head out slowly and I saw that the snake was alive, but it was no longer in the striking position. The snake was paralyzed. It could not move, as if the head was wounded. So, I crawled out and picked the snake up by the tail and showed the children that it could not harm them. The snake was completely paralyzed.

The Holy Spirit alerted me that the Devil was ready to make another move against me and the children represented the Lord's Church. About a week later, I pulled up to the Church during the week and in the parking lot, I noticed a circle of moldy baked bread placed very carefully with five loaves that made up the circle and two large loaves in the center. The Lord revealed to us that this was the demonic attack of witchcraft. The five loaves were meant to represent my siblings and I. and the two large loaves were supposed to represent our parents, our senior pastors. This is an attack on us and our ministry but remember the snake in the dream was paralyzed and couldn't move. My family gathered to pray and bind the enemy. We bound every fowl unclean spirit in the name of Jesus Christ.

In this warfare prayer, I remember sending that curse back to the sender by the fire of the Holy Spirit. Let me fill you in on something. When the enemy attacks our families and our church family, I take that very personal. This is war, and I will not show mercy to an enemy of that level. Here is how that specific prayer went.

> Heavenly Father, I thank you for the warning of this serpent. Lord, I glorify your Holy Name. I stand in the authority that you have given your Church. I will move in your name by faith.
>
> In the mighty name of Jesus Christ, I dismantle every demonic altar with my name on and my family's name on it and my ministry as well as the Lord's Church and His sheep (members) as well as their families.
>
> I send this curse back to the sender in the name of Jesus to be tormented by the very curse that they sent until they repent to the Lord for what they have done, in the name of Jesus Christ. I send back the flaming arrows that were sent our way and I dip them in the blood of Jesus Christ, and I send them back to this satanic camp now in Jesus' Name. I send confusion to the enemy's camp, and this witch will repent to the Lord or die, in Jesus' name.

You cannot back down. Power has been given to the Church by our savior Jesus Christ. A few months later I found out that the palm reader soothsayer that lived in the church neighborhood had died. The Lord will be with you in the fight.

As for the Devil's agent, the witch that was hired clearly made their choice, So I send back this spirit of death.

Many people will not understand the intensity in my prayers. I will say things like, "Choke slam the Devil," or "dip the arrows," or "make the Devil choke on the blood of Jesus." This is not Scripturally based, although it is from my experience of elevated warfare, and only the Word of God will defeat the enemy.

Another Snake

Recently, the Lord visited me again in another dream, in this dream I was getting into a golf cart. Then out of nowhere, I heard a voice that said, "Get out! Get out! There is a snake coiled up ready to strike on the dashboard!" I asked "Where? I don't see it!" The voice said, "It is directly in front of you. It blends into the cart. That's why you can't see it, but it is there." I never got out of the cart, as I prayed, "Lord, show me, where is this snake?" The Lord said, "I have paralyzed the snake. It cannot harm you." At that moment I looked between the dashboard and the windshield and there it was. Now it was stretched out across the front, alive and breathing but it couldn't move. This one had its tongue hanging out of its mouth.

I called my wife and my three sisters to talk about this dream. The Lord told me that the reason why I could not see the snake was that it blended in so well camouflaged to the cart that I was in, which means that it is someone within our inner circle that had been running their mouth about our family and ministry, but it wouldn't go any further. It wasn't just so close as part of the inner circle. The reason why I couldn't see it was that it was a "so-called believer in Christ" that was disguised as a Christian but was an agent of the Devil, trying to plant witchcraft and spread false rumors. This was an attack from the Devil, but through the gift of discerning spirits, the Lord showed me that he did not allow this enemy to succeed in any of its intentions against me or my family and ministry because the Lord paralyzed the Devil's works and guess what, a couple of weeks went by when the Lord exposed who that person was.

Here are a couple of verses for you to hold on to and put in your file of Holy Ghost arsenal prayers.

> Luke 10:19 KJV - Behold, I give unto you power to tread on serpents and scorpions, and over all the power of the enemy: and nothing shall by any means hurt you.

This verse shows us that the enemy may not retaliate against the Lord's church

> 1 John 3:8 KJV - He that committed sin is of the Devil, for the Devil sinneth from the beginning. For this purpose, the Son of God was manifested, so that He might destroy the works of the Devil.

Draw near to Jesus, my friend. The gates of hell will not prevail against the Lord's Church. We must be dressed daily in the full armor of God. Know that there is a whole other world around us, the spirit realm that the Lord is awakening His church to represent Him. There is so much more of the Lord available to the church of the Living God.

Know that you are loved far beyond what you could ever imagine. We must get out of our comfort zone and start reaching out to the people that we love; this is the best place to start. If they do not receive your invitation to Jesus, just keep praying for them. Don't get discouraged; just give them some space and continue prayers from a distance. Don't go at them with the strong-arm hammer pounding in your face method; just share with them what the Lord has done in your life. Keep it true and honest and know that the Lord will work in their heart. Pray against all stubborn spirits in the name of Jesus Christ and remember that the Lord is ready to clothe you in His righteousness. Congratulations! Your new life in Christ has begun.

Chapter 13

Serpents and Scorpions

A few nights ago, around four o'clock in the morning, I was having a dream. I was in a courtroom setting, but this was like a small old courtroom. I could see the area where the twelve jurors sit. However, there were just a few and only one of them stuck out like a sore thumb. It was as if I was about to question this person that was sitting in a chair in the juror's box. There were a few others in the box as well, but they were a blur, but the man who stuck out to me was just sitting there with his eyes wide open as if he had seen a ghost. I mean his eyes were very wide open, and he was just sitting there staring directly at me but wasn't saying anything, giving me just this cold stare. So, I turned my direction to him, and as I started to walk toward him. I could feel evil presence come over me as soon as we made eye contact with each other.

Now it was as if I was defending someone in this courtroom because I was moving toward him. As I was getting ready to open my mouth to speak, I locked eyes with him and he wouldn't even blink an eye, just a cold stare with both of his eyes wide open. I opened my mouth and pointed my finger toward him and to my surprise, nothing would come out of my mouth. This whole time he was just looking forward with his eyes wide open, so I recognized at once that this was a demonic spirit.

I then tried to speak the words, "I bind you in the name of Jesus," but the words wouldn't come out of my mouth. It was as if I was slurring struggling to speak each word, as I was trying very hard and I just couldn't form the words. As a cold chill went down my arms, I recognized this demon, so I started to move backward to get myself at a safe distance so that I could speak the words that I needed to because it was clear at this point that I was under a spiritual demonic attack. As I am about eight feet away, my voice started coming back to me and I was saying, "Jesus, Jesus, Jesus." As soon as I said Jesus the third time, I said, "I bind you in the name of Jesus Christ" As I started to move towards him again, I continued saying, "You lying Devil, I bind you, you deaf and dumb, spirit." Then I was close enough to the man that I couldn't speak again. The words once again wouldn't come out of my mouth.

Then I heard my wife. She gently woke me and asked, "Are you ok? You were mumbling in your sleep." I said, "Yes I am okay. I was in a spiritual battle with a demon. I was trying to bind him in the name of Jesus, but the words wouldn't come out of my mouth as I drew closer to him." I found myself engaged in this battle. As I lay in bed with my eyes open, I began to pray. This was my prayer:

> Father, in the name of Jesus, thank you for revealing this to me. I know that I was in a spiritual battle, but Lord, show me, what it means, the courtroom, the man with his eyes wide open. Lord, what was this? Who was this evil spirit? Lord, I know you are with me, and I wasn't backing down, but why did he still have power over me the closer I would get to him?

This was what the Lord said to me, "Satan is trying to silence you from praying for my people. This is taking place in my presence which becomes my courtroom when my people engage in warfare prayers. The reason he had power over your words is that he was trying hard to silence you, but it was I who pulled you back to regroup so you could speak. The enemy could control your speech because this kind requires prayer and fasting. Be in a spiritual fast when approaching chief demons." The Lord said, "I know that you are willing, but make sure that you prepare and are fully equipped."

I said, "Yes Lord, I was willing, but I was not ready. Lord, I will never stop praying for people. I will continue to lay hands on the sick, and I will continue to engage the enemy to defend the lost. Lord wherever you send me, I will go. Father, never leave me. I will walk by faith and not by sight. I will continue to move forward by faith in your Holy name. I have seen too much of your goodness, mercy, and love to back down from the counterfeit powers of the Devil."

> Mark 9:29 New King James Version - So, he said to them, "This kind can come out by nothing but prayer and fasting."

We must prepare ourselves for the spiritual battle. I need to be clear on this, and our focus should never be on what the enemy is trying to do. Our focus and full attention should always be on Jesus and what the Lord wants us to do. Spend quality time with the Lord. Please keep in mind that even though you may be willing, and you feel like you are strong in faith, all that is great, but always make sure that you have spent one-on-one time with the Lord through fasting, worship, and prayer. Remember, these are very powerful spiritual weapons that will open a can of the Holy Ghost whooping on the enemy.

A few nights ago, I was praying, and I was asking the Lord about the Bible verse Luke 10:19. I asked, "Why did you single out the snake and the scorpion? Lord, it must have a deeper spiritual meaning, deeper than what we have been taught. Please show me, so here is the verse I was asking Him about.

> Luke 10:19 KJV - Behold, I give unto you power to tread on serpents and scorpions, and over all the power of the enemy: and nothing shall by any means hurt you.

This is what the Lord showed me. He gave me a spiritual revelation and the understanding of the blueprint that the enemy uses concerning the serpent (snake) and the scorpion. This is what the Lord said to me. Let's first look at the characteristics of the snake.

There are two types of snakes, venomous and non-venomous. Nonvenomous snakes have two rows of teeth on the upper jaw and one row of teeth on the lower jaw. The teeth in these snakes face inwards to prevent their prey from escaping their grip. The other types of non-venomous snakes are different types of pythons that squeeze the life out of their prey.

Now, let's look at the venomous snakes. A venomous snake will inject venom into their prey and there are snakes like cobras that will spit their venom. The crazy thing about this snake is that it will aim for the eyes, to blind its enemy. Doesn't that sound to you like a move of the enemy? This is what the Lord showed me on this.

The enemy will use people in your circle to spit poison at you, to blind you to make you disoriented to truth. Or they will speak lies or gossip about someone or a situation, to get you mentally defeated by discouraging you in some way. Either way, you look at it, this is the poison that attacks the mind. All snakes shed their skin when they grow, if you feed the snake (demon) by believing the poison it will continue to grow and will shed its skin, starve them out. Don't feed your flesh, and feed your spirit. To be clear on this, the serpent with venom attacks your mind, also causing arguments, contention, bickering, quarreling, and fighting as it injects its poison into your mind.

This is the revelation the Lord gave me about Satan. This may challenge your faith, because it is the type of thinking that is "out of the box". God's ways are not our ways nor are His thoughts our thoughts. His way of thinking is much higher than ours. In the Bible, everything that has breath God refers to it as fruit. Even, as believers, the Bible says that we will be known by our fruit. Let's look at the verses in the proper context.

<u>Matthew 7:15-20</u>

> ***"You Will Know Them by Their Fruits"***
>
> 15) "Beware of false prophets, who come to you in sheep's clothing, but inwardly they are ravenous wolves.
>
> 16) You will know them by their fruits. Do men gather grapes from thornbushes or figs from thistles?
>
> 17) Even so, every good tree bears good fruit, but a bad tree bears bad fruit.
>
> 18) A good tree cannot bear bad fruit, nor can a bad tree bear good fruit.
>
> 19) Every tree that does not bear good fruit is cut down and thrown into the fire.
>
> 20) Therefore by their fruits you will know them.

You will know false prophets (people) by the type of (people) they produce. Notice how the false prophet can only produce his kind because there is no good in him. Therefore, he bears bad fruit. So, the bigger picture is that God's creation is fruit. It's either bad fruit or good fruit. The Lord showed me that Eve did not eat low-hanging fruit. Let's see what God told them about the tree of good and evil.

> Genesis 2:17 - but of the tree of the knowledge of good and evil you shall not eat, for in the day that you eat of it you shall surely die.

This is how the Lord broke it down. Look at the word "of" in "but of the tree of good and evil you shall not eat, for in the day that you eat of it you shall die." The Lord said, "I did not say 'do not eat *from* the tree,' because 'from' would mean that the tree produced the fruit. But I said, 'do not eat *of* the tree' meaning that something inhabited the tree. Satan himself was the forbidden fruit that Eve ate. Satan's words were the poison she ate."

I questioned the Lord, "But Lord, your Word clearly says that she ate the fruit." The Lord said, "What do you do on Sunday morning? You preach my Word, and the sheep eat the meat of my Word. Eve ate of the words of Satan. She believed and accepted his poisonous words, and then she went back and fed the words to Adam."

Now let's look at the python. This snake will move very slowly and is very Suttle, and very patient as it moves into position. It constricts and suffocates its prey with bone-crushing force, shutting down all internal organs and crushing the lungs and bones as there is no room for a breath, applying so much pressure that the prey becomes weak and lifeless.

Now, let's look at the description I just gave you of the dying prey in the spirit realm. This python serpent does not attack the mind as much as it focuses on the flesh giving a person feelings of suffocation, gasping for air, anxiety, fear, wheezing, coughing, emphysema, COPD, tightness of the chest, lung problems, heart attacks, strokes, (lack of oxygen to the brain). I can now connect spiritually when people ask for certain prayers.

We can bind the serpent causing all these different types of problems. Make listening to the Holy Spirit your priority. Don't start guessing and start calling out any demon you can think of in hopes of getting the right demon out. What if you are calling out the spirit of the python, but it's attacking the mind, then it would be a venomous snake, not a python. Don't try to be too smart for your own good. Instead, say "You lying devil, you serpent, I bind you now in the name of Jesus. Come out now, and never return. I cast you bound and muzzled to the feet of Jesus Christ to await your judgment fire from God, and you may not pass your assignment to any other demonic spirit and you may never return to this bloodline in the name of Jesus Christ. Amen."

The Scorpion has eight legs, and two pedipalps with a venom-injecting barb on its tail. The scorpion has two venom glands like the snake. It doesn't have any bones. However, it has an exoskeleton like the shell of a shrimp. It glows in the dark and eats just about anything. The scorpion is the symbol of death, evil, poison, and unpleasantness.

Revelation 9:1-10 KJV

> 1) And the fifth angel sounded, and I saw a star fall from heaven unto the earth: and to him was given the key of the bottomless pit.
>
> 2) And he opened the bottomless pit; and there arose a smoke out of the pit, as the smoke of a great furnace; and the sun and the air were darkened by reason of the smoke of the pit.
>
> 3) And there came out of the smoke locusts upon the earth: and unto them was given power, as the scorpions of the earth have power.
>
> 4) And it was commanded them that they should not hurt the grass of the earth, neither any green thing, neither any tree; but only those men who have not the seal of God in their foreheads.
>
> 5) And to them, it was given that they should not kill them, but that they should be tormented five months: and their torment was as the torment of a scorpion, when he striketh a man.
>
> 6) And in those days shall men seek death and shall not find it; and shall desire to die, and death shall flee from them.
>
> 7) And the shapes of the locusts were like unto horses prepared unto battle; and on their heads were as it were crowns like gold, and their faces were as the faces of men.

> 8) And they had hair as the hair of women, and their teeth were as the teeth of lions.
>
> 9) And they had breastplates, as it were breastplates of iron; and the sound of their wings was as the sound of chariots of many horses running to battle.
>
> 10) And they had tails like unto scorpions, and there were stings in their tails: and their power was to hurt men five months.

The role of the scorpion is not to kill you, but to torment you, to make you live unhappy, sick, and discouraged. Think about this. Its purpose is to inflict pain to the flesh of its prey. Have you ever been minding your own business when suddenly a sharp pain hits your knees? Or shoulders or your back locks up? The wiles of the enemy are to hit you when your spiritual guard is down. Where do you think these types of ailments come from along with bone aches, migraine headaches, muscle aches, and pains?

Or you suddenly feel anxious, and depression starts to close in taking you into isolation? These tormenting spirits are on the move against you, even bringing a certain hurt from the past that may have traumatized you. Now all the sudden memories from many years back are haunting you again. These demons are spreading their toxicity all over the believers in Jesus Christ. They are having a field day with the modern-day Church because today's Church is stuck in tradition or mistaking a talented worship team as anointed when they were just in the clubs playing weekend gigs. The Church has become powerless and defeated for lack of the Holy Spirit and sound doctrine at the pulpits.

Friend, the times here on this earth are only going to get worse and if you are not grounded in the word of God and have the gifts and the fruit of the Holy Spirit, you won't survive what is coming. The blood of Jesus Messiah along with your testimony of God's Word, grace, mercy, and power will defeat the enemy. These spirits are from the marine kingdom of Satan. Let me show you something that you may not have thought of. Remember, this will challenge your tradition and your faith. If you research horoscope and astrology, you will find that they are satanic.

Let's look at Scorpio, one of the water signs. The ones that are compatible with Scorpio are Cancer and Pisces. It is a fixed negative sign. Cancer itself is self-explanatory just in its name. This demon of cancer causes all kinds of cancer in the blood, bones, brain, liver, intestines, or any other part of the body. These evil spirits work together to destroy us. Scorpio is the scorpion, also being a water symbol.

Now let's take a closer look at Pisces, the symbol for which is a fish. These demons work through dreams and a person's emotions. You don't have to believe in them for them to exist. They exist. Stand against them in Christ Jesus to defeat them. Notice its symbol is a fish, also from the waters. These zodiac symbols are all demonic. These are immobilizing spirits assigned to destroy us and our families. Do you see how the enemy attacks? Now, let me show you the Bible verse that will take place during the great tribulation period when Satan is once and for all kicked out of heaven. Remember, at this moment he is in God's ear accusing the brethren, but the time is coming when he will be cast out of the third heaven onto this earth to join his marine kingdom.

> Revelation 12:12 KJV - Therefore rejoice, ye heavens, and ye that dwell in them. Woe to the inhabiters of the earth and of the sea! for the Devil is come down unto you, having great wrath, because he knoweth that he hath but a short time.

Look at it again. Woe to the inhabitants of the earth and the sea. This is the marine kingdom, and it is very real. You must not be afraid; however, it is crucial for the Church, (that's you) to buck down and prepare yourself and your loved ones for the spiritual battle that is on the rise. You must remember that you have been given power and authority over this demonic kingdom through Jesus Christ. As a believer in Jesus Christ, invite and welcome the Holy Spirit into your life and never back down from any of these spiritual enemies. The giants come down hard and the mountains will move when you activate the Spirit of God that Jesus Christ deposited inside of you when you accepted Him as truth in your life and to be your personal Lord and Savior.

Now you have a better idea of the enemy's playbook. You know who and what these demonic snakes and scorpions plan to do. Now, you must get dressed in the full armor of God and submit to Him. Resist the Devil and he will flee. But it doesn't end there. Remember, you also have power over all, which means the rest of his power. You can overrule his plans against you and his power. "Man your battle station," and be on high alert. Pray and fast and thank the Lord. Position yourself for victory. I bless you in the name of Jesus Christ.

Chapter 14

Letting Go of The Past

As we near the end of this book, I would like to acknowledge the reality that change can be an uncomfortable place to be in one's life. However, at the rapid rate this whole world is changing, we must understand that things will not get much better. We must accept that the life and the times we lived as children are behind us. I grew up in the 1980s when we kids used to ride our bikes outside in the summertime all day long. We knew that it was time to come home when the corner streetlight would turn on. But the direction that this world is going is very uncomfortable.

One day I stopped at a gas station and as I was walking inside the store, I noticed a young lady walking just behind me. She may have been in her early twenties. So, as I approached the door, I reached out and pulled the door open to let her walk through before me. Well, don't you know that she stopped and said to me, "You go ahead and go in, I can hold my own door, thank you!" with a smug attitude. I said, "okay," and walked in. She then commented, "The nerve, as if I'm a weak woman and can't open my door." I thought to myself, these kids don't know anything about manners or respect. I was upset but in a disappointed kind of way. So, I prayed about it, and this is how the Lord broke this down for me so that I would not harbor any type of hatred or bitterness.

The Lord said to me, "Do you remember when you were a child, your family had a 1979 station wagon?" I said, "Yes Lord, I remember that old station wagon." Then the Lord said, "That was not an old station wagon at the time. But cars back then did not come with the features that today's vehicles come with. You learned how to appreciate the features in today's vehicles because in your day as a child, there was no backup camera; there were no seat warmers; there was no blind spot monitoring system; and there was no Bluetooth for a phone.

"You did not have these as a child. It was to your generation that I gave these ideas for safety. But Satan has corrupted these features and uses things like phones to take lives while a person is driving. But to your generation, these are nice features to have but you can do without them because you didn't always have them.

"To a younger person, they do not appreciate the features because they have always had them; they don't understand what it is like *not to have* air conditioning; all they know is that it needs to work. They don't know about not having the features; all they know is that they are supposed to work. They do not know how to do without. Therefore, they believe that they are entitled to the very best.

"Just like your country, the United States of America, they don't understand their freedom. They just believe that they are entitled to that freedom because they were born into it. They do not understand that someone had to fight, someone had to sacrifice, and someone had to die for their freedom. Therefore, you must teach about my grace, my mercy, my death, and my resurrection. They are not entitled to the freedom I have to offer. They will not inherit your faith; I must work it out in them individually. I had to die for them to walk in my goodness."

The features of salvation through Jesus Christ come free to this world, but our Lord had to suffer so we could have the best of life in Him and with Him in our lives have His peace, grace, mercy, His redemption, and forgiveness of sins. These features come in the renewed mind of the person that has died to sin and accepted the Lord as their personal Savior. They are in the benefits package of a true child of God, along with eternal life with Christ, His Holy Spirit, the nine gifts of the Holy

Spirit, the fire of His Spirit along with the fruit of the Holy Spirit. That is evidence of a renewed mind and character.

The Lord also put in my heart to cherish the times of the way things once were, but for me to not grow angry or bitter in the direction this world is going, I must embrace Him. He is my peace and must be my place of refuge. You must do the same. Keep the memories that are worth keeping in your heart and discard the rest. Keep in mind that what you discard is waste; it's dead weight. You don't need to carry useless heaviness into your new day of tomorrow.

Take a moment to thank the Lord for what He has done. Thank Him for what He is going to do and for what He didn't do as well as what He won't do. The Lord, and only the Lord, knows what is best for you. Friend, prepare your life spiritually. Troubled times are coming to our homeland. The bible has made this clear to us that the whole world will crumble underneath us, and the governments of this world will fall apart. Prepare yourself now for worldwide famine.

The country, as I am writing this, is on the verge of a financial recession. The governments of the world are pushing towards the 2030 agenda. They call it the great reset. My point is, Jesus is our only place of refuge. We must teach our children and all our loved ones how to pray and how to trust in God. We must learn and teach them about the truth that the Father, the Son, and the Holy Spirit all three are one. Some of us want to be used by God, but we aren't willing to examine ourselves. We must always have a repentant heart. There are many things in our own lives that we just won't let go of. We must learn the word of God because one day this world will outlaw the Holy Bible. The Word of God must be in our hearts, not just on our lips. We must prepare spiritually, stop playing church, and turn our zeal to work for God into faith.

The way you stop doing the "I want to do this or that for the Lord" is like this: "Lord, what do you want me to do? Show me which way to go and what to say. I am moving by faith, Lord. Holy Spirit direct my path." Turn your zeal into faith and start moving in the name of Jesus. The Lord will be walking with you, so be sure you are in constant communication with Him. But remember to be quiet long enough to allow Him to respond to you. As you are moving, He will be moving with you. There is just too much to do and many souls to reach for the Kingdom of Heaven is at hand.

Here is one major key to you letting go of the past and allowing yourself to move forward. You must separate your emotional attachments from your spiritual needs and requirements. Separate the emotions from past soul ties, past relationships, habits of the past, and the life you once lived. Release and break free from people or even memories of people who are holding your spiritual walk with Christ hostage. These things are not allowing you to move forward with your life. You must sever those ties in the name of Jesus. There is a woman in the Bible that wouldn't let go and it led to her destruction. We know her as Lots wife. Let's take a close look at this in the Bible. This is when the two angels arrived at Lot's house. We will break it down as the Lord showed me as we go.

<u>Genesis 18:17-19 KJV</u>

> 17) And the Lord said, Shall I hide from Abraham that thing which I do;
>
> 18) Seeing that Abraham shall surely become a great and mighty nation, and all the nations of the earth shall be blessed in him?
>
> 19) For I know him, that he will command his children and his household after him, and they shall keep the way of the Lord, to do justice and judgment; that the Lord may bring upon Abraham that which he hath spoken of him.

So, what we are seeing in this passage is that for Abraham to become a great nation of people all over the world, Abraham's household would expand. Justice and judgement had to erase Sodom and Gomorrah because their sins were great, and they refused to repent. This judgement had to come so Abraham's prophecy, that which had been spoken of him. The reason God decided to tell Abraham about the destruction of Sodom was that part of the promise to Abraham was that his descendants were directly involved, "I will make you a great Nation." I believe that Lot and his family represent you and me, being the Church in this story. Abraham is a type of Christ. While God is speaking to the angels concerning Lot, we are about to see that the two men (angels) turn and leave Lot and head for Sodom to begin their assignment.

Genesis 18:22-24 KJV

> 22) And the men turned their faces from thence and went toward Sodom: but Abraham stood yet before the Lord.
>
> 23) And Abraham drew near, and said, wilt thou also destroy the righteous with the wicked?
>
> 24) Peradventure there be fifty righteous within the city: wilt thou also destroys and not spare the place for the fifty righteous that are therein?

This is what I find to be so amazing. Abraham is not praying for his nephew. He is speaking one on one with God. He is pleading with God for his nephew. The Lord knew that there weren't any righteous people in Sodom or Gomorrah, but the Lord was patient with him. Abraham started at fifty righteous and asked the Lord "If you find fifty righteous people, will you destroy the righteous with the wicked?" Abraham negotiated with the Lord all the way from fifty righteous down to ten righteous.

This is what you must know about your prayers. As Abraham is talking with the Lord, the two angels have already been assigned and dispatched to his nephew Lot. This should show you that while you are praying for your loved ones God is already there. Angels have already been assigned and are on the move on your behalf because of your personal relationship with the Lord. Just like Abraham's nephew was not a righteous man, nor was his family, doesn't mean that God won't eventually save them. Here is the main reason why. Just as Lot was connected to Abraham through blood, we are connected to Christ through His blood. Don't stop praying. You must not stop pleading with the Lord for your lost loved ones.

The best evidence of God's mercy in this story is that Abraham didn't know that the angels were already with his nephew, Lot and his family. Lot had no idea that his uncle Abraham was pleading with God for him and his family. There are certain things we just can't see, and that is why we should walk by faith and not by sight. As these two men have made their way to Lot, he recognized them as angels. Lot offered to feed them and wash their feet and insisted that they stay with him in his house. But they wanted to stay in the streets to observe the city, and how the people would receive them. Lot knew that would be a very bad idea, not for the two men, but the city and all the people in the city.

<u>Genesis 19:4-7 KJV</u>

4) But before they lay down, the men of the city, even the men of Sodom, compassed the house round, both old and young, all the people from every quarter:

5) And they called unto Lot, and said unto him, where are the men which came into thee this night? Bring them out unto us, that we may know them.

What they were saying is that they wanted to sexually rape and molest the men. (the angels) These people were so wicked. You must remember that the word wicked means to be immoral. This is dirty and filthy wickedness at its best. It is the Devil at work.

> 6) And Lot went out at the door unto them, and shut the door after him,
>
> 7) And said, I pray you, brethren, do not so wickedly.

So, now we can see that Lot is doing everything he can to protect the two men, but at some point, you must stop and ask yourself, "Does Lot know that these two men are angels at this point? Or does he think these are just two men that came to visit him?" Either way, he chooses to look at these two men. Something serious is about to go down. I have often wondered about how Lot viewed these men. But now we are about to get even deeper into this story, and we will get to the core of this whole chapter about letting go of the past. You are about to see why I picked this biblical story to connect with you on this specific topic. Let's dive into the next verse.

> 8) Behold now, I have two daughters which have not known man; let me, I pray you, bring them out unto you, and do ye to them as is good in your eyes: only unto these men do nothing; for therefore came they under the shadow of my roof.

There is our proof that Lot was not a righteous man. You would have to stop and ask yourself, "What kind of father would offer his daughter to a community of men, to rape his daughters and do whatever they wanted to do to them and be ok with it?" This is true wickedness, but God is still there. Now you're probably asking yourself why is God still wanting to rescue Lot and his family. It is because of Abraham's relationship with the Lord, a promise from God that must be fulfilled.

This is what I am telling you today. Perhaps the people you are praying for do not know the Lord, but you love them, or they are connected to you through blood. God will still honor your prayers; this is the grace and mercy of our Lord because none of us could ever earn such love and mercy.

> 9) And they said, Stand back. And they said again, this one fellow came into sojourn, and he will needs be a judge: now will we deal worse with thee, than with them. And they pressed sore upon the man, even Lot, and came near to break the door.

Such wickedness in the men of this community, they had him cornered and began to threaten his life and to do worse to him than they were going to do to the two men. Since the angels are on assignment to save Lot, they had to get Lot to safety and pull him back into the house. This is what I was telling you in an earlier chapter that in Christ you have the power to send our warring angels to change the outcome of a person or people's life. The Lord sends out the order and the angels must obey the divine order.

> 10) But the men put forth their hand, and pulled Lot into the house to them, and shut to the door.
>
> 11) And they smote the men that were at the door of the house with blindness, both small and great: so that they wearied themselves to find the door.
>
> They wearied themselves to find the door, they are so blinded by their wickedness that they are still tripping over each other trying to find the door to feed their lustful flesh.
>
> 12) And the men said unto Lot, Hast thou here any besides? Son in law, and thy sons, and thy daughters, and whatsoever thou hast in the city, bring them out of this place:

> 13) For we will destroy this place because the cry of them is waxen great before the face of the Lord; and the Lord hath sent us to destroy it.

This is cool. Their cries to God had waxen great before the face of the Lord, which means just like many believers today that are in church, but the church isn't in them. This means their cries are like a wax figure. It looks real, and they have a form of godliness but deny the power thereof. Their cries to God are fake, not from the heart. This is a lesson for us that our cries to the Lord must be wholehearted. God will not receive fake worship, nor fake praise, nor will He hear fake cries. We must always have a heart of repentance. We can see that Lot loves his family, he goes out and speaks to his sons-in-law to get ready to leave because destruction was coming, but they didn't believe him. This is the saddest part of this whole story that we can relate to. Many of us have loved ones that don't listen to us when we try to tell them about the last days that we are living in right now. The Devil is working so hard in this world to debunk the rapture of the church, and he is trying to say that the Bible is fake, and people are buying into this wicked deception.

> 14) And Lot went out, and spoke unto his sons in law, which married his daughters, and said, Up, get you out of this place; for the Lord will destroy this city. But he seemed as one that mocked unto his sons in law.
>
> 15) And when the morning arose, then the angels hastened Lot, saying, Arise, take thy wife, and thy two daughters, which are here; lest thou be consumed in the iniquity of the city.
>
> 16) And while he lingered, the men laid hold upon his hand, and upon the hand of his wife, and upon the hand of his two daughters; the Lord being merciful unto him: and they brought him forth and

> set him without the city.

This is the part of the story that is always overlooked. Now we are getting to the meat of this story. Notice how Lot spoke with his sons-in-law, and they didn't believe him. These scriptures also tell us that those sons-in-law were married to Lot's other daughters, he even had grown sons that lived in the city. This is not counting the two daughters that were living at home that lost respect for him when he offered them to the men of the city. So, we just read that the angels told him to get his wife and two daughters and leave now! But Lot lingered.

I don't blame Lot for lingering. He was waiting for his children to arrive so they can all leave together. This is a clear picture of the rapture when the Lord comes back for his church, many of us are praying for our loved ones like Abraham, and many of us won't commit our lives to the Lord like Lot, and some of us just won't believe that that day is coming like Lots other children.

> 17) And it came to pass, when they had brought them forth abroad, that he said, escape for thy life; look not behind thee, neither stay thou in all the plain; escape to the mountain, lest thou be consumed.
>
> 18) And Lot said unto them, Oh, not so, my Lord:

There it is my friend. Don't look back! And don't even stay in the area. we know that Jesus Christ is our mountain. He is our place of refuge. He is our Ark. When you read this again carefully notice that the angels are having to force Lot and his wife to leave, but they don't want to leave, because they are waiting for their loved ones. However, the angels' warning is clear, "If you don't move forward to the mountain, and if you look back on your past, the life you love, the life you lived, and everyone in that life, it will keep you bound mentally and won't allow you to move forward. It will consume you."

19) Behold now, thy servant hath found grace in thy sight, and thou hast magnified thy mercy, which thou hast shewed unto me in saving my life; and I cannot escape to the mountain, lest some evil take me, and I die:

20) Behold now, this city is near to flee unto, and it is a little one: Oh, let me escape thither, (is it not a little one?) and my soul shall live.

21) And he said unto him, See, I have accepted thee concerning this thing also, that I will not overthrow this city, for the which, thou hast spoken.

22) Haste thee, escape thither; for I cannot do anything till thou become thither. Therefore, the name of the city was called Zoar.

We notice that Lot knows of a city to which he can escape, and they are headed that way, but listen to what the angel said, "Lot you must come now because I can't do what I was sent to do until you start moving toward me." If you truly want a new life in Christ, your new life isn't going to just fall out of the sky into your lap. You need to start making spiritual moves toward the Lord. Your mind must be made up to follow Jesus and you cannot hold on to the past, you must let it go!

23) The sun was risen upon the earth when Lot entered Zoar.

24) Then the Lord rained upon Sodom and upon Gomorrah brimstone and fire from the Lord out of heaven.

25) And he overthrew those cities, and all the plain, and all the inhabitants of the cities, and that which grew upon the ground.

26) But his wife looked back from behind him, and she became a pillar of salt.

We are here. Do you need to take a moment to get a glass of water or get up and walk around? Here we go! Please keep in mind that they are being forced to leave. The prayers of his uncle Abraham had sent out the divine order of the Lord to dispatch the angels on a mission to save Lot and his family. As they are running for their lives, we see that Lot's wife looked back and became a pillar of salt. I don't blame her for looking back. Notice that she didn't glance back, she looked back, she is broken, her babies didn't come because their husbands didn't believe Lot, so they are dying, as well as her sons. She could hear the cries of all the people in the city and she was looking at the destruction, the homes of all their friends, all of the people of the city. She was looking at all of this while hearing their cries. She was consumed. Her heart was still there. She became what she loved more than God, a pillar of salt, the judgment of God consumed her because she would not let go and move toward God. My friend do not let this happen to you. Please share this story with your children and their families. Now is the time to come to Jesus Christ because the Lord will soon return. Lot's daughter told their husband something like, "You see we should have listened to Dad, and we should have left with them!" Think about it. When the ash started to fall, they may have still been able to leave. But pride will keep you bound and it will keep you from making a change. Pride is of the Devil. Don't let the Devil get in your way.

One can look at this world and know that something is different and the times of life have changed. We the Church must be in prayer like never before. It is time to let go of the past, let go of old ways of doing things, let go of old habits, let go of the hurtful memories, let go of certain toxic people, and don't let memories keep you bound; you must break away.

You must run toward Jesus for shelter and bring all your loved ones with you. My friend, we are all running out of time to reach them. Don't let the Devil use your past to consume you. You must mentally and emotionally sever the ties that hold you to your past. It will be a process, however; at least the process of healing will be set in motion. I will help you with a prayer to pray to the Lord. However, it will be up to you to start moving toward Jesus in your everyday life. I bless you and your family in the name of Jesus Christ.

PRAYER

Heavenly Father,

I am asking for your help at this time in my life. I realize that I have sinned against you my whole life. I have hurt that I have held onto, and I have memories that I haven't let go of. I want you to be the Lord of my Life and I don't want these things to keep me bound and to get in the way of my healing and restoration through you. Lord, even what people have done to me and what I have done to others, please forgive me. I need your help daily, to show me how to release this to you, and even show me how to forgive myself.

Lord, I am willing and only you can make me able. I chose to forgive all who have hurt and offended me, and Lord, please forgive me for hurting and offending others. Teach me to see you and teach me to hear your voice. Give me your love and change my character. I need strength, I will draw this power from your love for me.

Lord, I surrender to your will for my life. Lord, please send angels to my loved ones, please show them mercy. Lord, please spare their souls. Lord, my family is not walking with you, but neither was Lot and because of your relationship and promise to Abraham you spared his family. Lord please do it for me and my loved ones. Lord, please help us all. In Jesus Christ's name, I pray.

Amen.

Chapter 15

"LOVE"

In conclusion, I want to talk with you about the fruit of the Spirit, LOVE. Love is the source from which we draw the power, strength, and courage when we find ourselves in our low points and high points in life. The seed of the Gospel that we believe in is love centered. Keep in mind that this isn't the emotion of love; this is the fruit, the character of the Holy Spirit. This world is only going to get tougher, and that is perfectly okay. This is the way God has told us the way it will be. You were created for this time in life. So, I have put this breakdown together for you the way the Lord gave it to me.

When the seed of the word is planted, the enemy comes to rob the seed. The seed of the Gospel is LOVE.

Perfect love transforms one's character. Here is a description of love in the Holy Bible.

1 Corinthians 13:4-8

> 4) Love is patient, love is kind. It does not envy, it does not boast, it is not proud.
>
> 5) It does not dishonor others, it is not self-seeking, it is not easily angered, it keeps no record of wrongs.
>
> 6) Love does not delight in evil but rejoices with the truth.
>
> 7) It always protects, always trusts, always hopes, always perseveres.
>
> 8) Love never fails. But where there are prophecies, they will cease; where there are tongues, they will be stilled; where there is

> knowledge, it will pass away.

Love will not dishonor, does not envy, does not boast, is not prideful, is not self-seeking, is not easily angered, does not hold grudges, and never fails. Love is the source from which we draw strength. Think about it. We draw power from the virtue of Christ Jesus. This fuels the inner spirit that lights us back up. If you need a more tangible source, then think of your testimony.

The Lord didn't bring you this far to allow you to go down in shame. He didn't teach us to swim just to let us drown. No. He is with you. Remember, how God has saved you from so much. Think about His goodness and mercy in your life that revives your inner spirit using your testimony. Draw power from your testimony. Think on these things, the troubles you are going through; shake them off of you. Set yourself above these things. See yourself inside of the love of God and surrender to His love for you. Please keep in mind that this is not the emotion of love that we are discussing; this is the character of true love; this is the very nature of the person of the Holy Spirit.

<u>Galatians 5:22-23 KJV</u>

> 22) But the fruit of the Spirit is love, joy, peace, forbearance, kindness, goodness, faithfulness,
>
> 23) Gentleness and self-control. Against such things, there is no law.

As read, more we see that it is the FRUIT of the Spirit not fruits. Here is why. If I had a bowl of fresh fruit displayed on my table and you came to my house to visit, I would offer you some fruit. I wouldn't say, "Would you like fresh fruits?" No, I would say, "Have some fruit," because it is all of the same although they are individually, uniquely different. They all work together to represent its kind.

In other words, I can't make oranges out of apple seeds, and I can't make bananas out of strawberry seeds, yet they are all still fruit. So, this takes us back to the seed of its kind, and the seed of the Gospel is love and love is a picture of the Lord Himself and His love will change your life. But you must remember that there will be opposition when this happens, the enemy will come to rob the seed of the Gospel.

The Devil cannot create anything. God is the creator. All the Devil does is corrupt; he corrupts the good seed and makes it sinfully wicked. When we take the time to break this all down, we will see that the seed of the Gospel is love because without love we have nothing.

> 1 Corinthians 13:1 - Though I speak with the tongues of men and of angels, (but have not love,) I have become sounding brass or a clanging cymbal.

Love is the key. Love is the seed and inside of love is the blueprint for joy, peace, patience, kindness, goodness, faithfulness, gentleness, and self-control. Did you notice that He said in that verse "Though I speak with the tongue of men and angels?" One cannot speak in tongues the language of angels without the baptism of the Holy Spirit. That means that there are ministers and fellow Christians going around laying hands on people for prayer and going through the motions of "what we are supposed to do" but lacking the main ingredient, which is love.

Therefore, it is important for you and me to be honest with ourselves and do some serious self-evaluation of the true motives of our hearts. We all should be motivated by the love and compassion of the Lord, to effectively represent Him. One cannot walk around, going through the motions, and expect to be effective. Many of us lack the very things we are praying for others to receive through our prayers.

How can we effectively pray for someone to receive peace from God if we lack the peace of God in our own lives? If I can't believe it for myself, then how could I believe it for someone else? That is simply because we don't have peace because we don't have the love of God. We get so caught up in searching for the peace of God when we should have the God of peace in us. We shouldn't have to search so hard. The Lord is right there in you. We don't have the joy of the Lord because we don't have His love. Remember that the seed of the Gospel is love, and inside of the seed of love is the blueprint for joy, peace, patience, longsuffering, kindness, forbearance, and faithfulness. We lack compassion for the lost, for the suffering, for the weary simply because we lack love.

The fruit of the tree of life is love. The Lord placed two trees in the middle of the garden: the tree of life and the tree of knowledge of good and evil. Let's look at this through spiritual eyes. The tree of life had the fruit of love (Jesus) hanging on it, while the tree of knowledge of good and evil had deception and pride on it. Get dressed in the armor of God; get dressed in righteousness because we wear whom we partner with.

> John 3:16 - for God so LOVED the world, that He gave his only begotten Son, that whosoever believes in Him should not perish but have ever lasting life.

The seed of the gospel is love and this blueprint will change your character. I could continue with a Scripture about God's love because the entire Bible is filled with stories of God's love for His people. But I am not going to do that just yet, I am going to start this chapter with something very personal to me in hopes that it may help you the way that it helped me.

Here is my confession to you. About ten years ago someone asked me a simple question. They asked, "Do you love the Lord with all of your heart and soul?" I said the obvious, safe answer, "Yes." Here is where my mind started spinning for days. The next few words that came out of his mouth were, "Then why do you hate yourself so much?" The smile was instantly wiped right off my face as for a moment, everything slowed down as I thought. I could almost feel the temples on the sides of my head pulsating. I fumbled for words. I simply had to confess the truth. I replied, "I'll have to get back to you on that later."

This simple question hit me hard. It shook my insides so much that I couldn't sleep for the next few days. So, I decided to do some research of my own. I needed to find out if God loved me and how I know that I truly loved Him. Don't get me wrong I have never doubted that God is real because I have seen God work in my life and the lives of my family members at a very young age. What I needed to know was, "How real am I?" I needed to get to the core of my inner being. I wanted to be searched by God, but at the same time, I was being very careful about how I was asking God to search me because I fear the Lord and didn't want to put myself in a position that I may regret.

God could very well humble me in a way that I am not sure I could handle. The way I went about it was I asked the Lord for His help, and I put myself under the spiritual microscope. I first started searching for His love for me. I needed to know how real my God's love for me is. You see we all grow up believing in something because it's what we are taught, "It's the right thing to do." But the fact is we believe the way we believe while we are growing up because this is what we are told to believe. But the major problem with that is when we grow up and our "religion" isn't comforting us or providing real answers for us, we end up going on a spiritual quest to "find ourselves." I will give you an example of what I mean.

One day I was in my car with a very close friend of mine. We were driving on the highway. We so happened to pass up a church, and he did the sign of the cross over himself and then kissed his fingers. I was very curious, so I asked him this sincere question, "What are you doing? What does that mean?" He gave me a straight look and hesitated a few seconds then said, "I don't know! This is what I was taught to do, so I do it out of respect." I asked, "Do you think you are talking to God? Because if you think that you are talking to God, you're not saying anything." He replied, "Well, if I don't know what it means then I guess it doesn't mean anything."

That right there is my point with this chapter. If we say that we believe in God the Father, God the Son, and God the Holy Spirit, then wouldn't you agree that we need to know what and who we believe in? Of course, we should. For us to know what we believe, we must have an understanding of our salvation through Christ, which all goes back to the cross; what Jesus did for us at Calvary and why He did it. The first thing to see is that it was God the father's love for us that started everything, and Christ was being obedient to the Father's will. So, we will start here with this Bible verse.

> John 3:16 - For God so loved the world, that he gave his only begotten son, that whosoever believes in him, will not perish but have everlasting life.

This verse starts with God the Father's Love for us. This is the very reason God the Father sent His Son. It was because He loves us. It is up to us to believe in His Son Jesus Christ. It is through Christ we can have eternal life because Christ conquered death. If we are in Christ and obedient to His will, we will have eternal life with Him in His kingdom. There is so much more available to us through Christ, and we have yet to tap into the Lord's grace and experience the fullness of His love.

A Desperation to See Jesus

One Bible story I love is of the woman who was desperate to see Jesus. She had made up her mind that if she could only make her way to Jesus and touch His cloak, she would be healed. With love in His eyes, Jesus looked down and saw her trembling with fear. Jesus reached down to her and helped her to her feet and told her that her faith had healed her. With love in His eyes, looking deep into her soul, Jesus set her free of her illness. Here is the story of that encounter.

Luke 8:43-48 KJV

> 43) And a woman having an issue of blood twelve years, which had spent all her living upon physicians, neither could be healed of any,
>
> 44) Came behind him and touched the border of his garment: and immediately her issue of blood stanched.
>
> 45) And Jesus said, who touched me? When all denied, Peter and they that were with him said, Master, the multitude throng thee and press thee, and sayest thou, who touched me?
>
> 46) And Jesus said, somebody hath touched me: for I perceive that virtue is gone out of me.
>
> 47) And when the woman saw that she was not hid, she came trembling and falling down before him, she declared unto him before all the people for what cause she had touched him, and how she was healed immediately.
>
> 48) And he said unto her, Daughter be of good comfort: thy faith hath made thee whole; go in peace.

I am blown away by this, Jesus felt virtue leave His body. Let's look at the definition of what *virtue* is.

Virtue is goodness, righteousness, morality, integrity, honor, nobility, worthiness, principles, purity and so much more.

This is so awesome. Jesus felt his virtue leave His body. What I find amazing is that the crowd was so thick that this woman had to crawl on her knees through the crowd to get to Jesus. She didn't even touch His body; she only touched the border of his garment. The level of her faith and desperation is what I relate to. We need to have that type of faith and most importantly we should have that hunger and desperation for more of Him.

This woman just knew that if she could reach even his garment, she would instantly be healed. Not a trace of doubt was in her faith. She knew that no matter what, she had to get to Jesus. This is where we miss it. Jesus should be in our hearts. He is with us. He is at the church, and He is at the Bible study. These are places where we don't have to fight the crowds to get to Him. He is right there waiting for us. But for some reason, we won't get off the couch on Sunday to go see Him and worship Him. We call it "family day" or "game day" and stay home or go out to play golf or go fishing on a Sunday. He is waiting for us, but we aren't desperate to have a holy encounter with our Savior.

Of course, we will rush to buy front row tickets to see our favorite artists and pay even more to meet them and take a picture with them so we can show our friends we were there. But to come and see Jesus right now is 100% free. This is what I can't understand. Like that woman, we need to find our way to Jesus no matter what. She fought through a crowd. The crowd we must fight through is mostly spiritual. It's what we struggle with most, things like doubt, fear, intimidation, anxiety, depression and more. Fight against what is keeping you bound. Fight it! Don't give up! Make your way to church this week more than once. Go see Jesus; He's waiting for you as we speak.

His love for you is beyond measure. Think about it. God the Father loved you first. He sent His Son Jesus to die on the cross for our sins. Jesus was here on a mission and had to be obedient to the Father's will. I love the way Jesus responded to the woman in this story. The other thing that blows me away is the silent detail of this story. For instance, let's look at it through our spiritual eyes. This woman had a blood issue for twelve years. Let's look at these two main facts.

First we have a "blood Issue". We know that this is a discharge, and the book of Leviticus gives us more insight on this issue.

> Leviticus 15:1, 2, 3 KJV - The Lord said to Moses and Aaron, speak to the Israelites and say to them, "When any man has a bodily discharge is unclean, whether it continues flowing from his body or is blocked, it will make him unclean. This is how his discharge will bring him about uncleanliness.
>
> Leviticus 15:19 - When a woman has her regular flow of blood, the impurity of her monthly period will last her seven days and anyone who touches her will be unclean until evening.

We see that this is referring to "uncleanliness and impurity." The spiritual meaning behind this story is that this woman was unclean, meaning by her sins. Because a blood discharge is dead blood. The blood of Jesus is living blood, and He is the living water. So, we see that her blood issue represented her sins.

Now, let's look at the twelve years. The number 12 in the Bible is also considered to represent completion. Let's take a quick look at some Biblical examples of the number 12.

Jacob had 12 sons, and each represented a tribe that began with 12 Princes. In the book of Leviticus, God specified that 12 cakes of unleavened bread were to be placed in the Temple. Remember that Jesus picked 12 disciples. We also see that in the Old Testament that

12,000 (twelve thousand) from each tribe of Israel were to complete the 144,000 total. Revelation 12 mentions that the church wears a crown containing 12 stars. The New Jerusalem, which is made in heaven and brought to the earth by God has 12 gates. These are a few biblical examples.

I said all of that to say it was time for this woman to have an encounter with Jesus Christ. Her 12 (completed) years had expired that very day. Perhaps your time has come. Maybe your time of suffering has come to an end? But as long as you stay in the same old day-after-day routine you will never know. Just like this woman, I am sure that she felt scared, but because she believed and stepped out in faith and acted on her faith and desperation, the Lord honored her faith. Because of her sins, she lacked virtue, but she had faith. I am saying to you right now if you have faith, God will give you what you are lacking to complete you. He will provide the virtue that you need because He is the only one who can. Friend, come to Jesus right now. Your time is here and now. You have the Lord's attention. He is looking at you asking, "Who touched me?" He wants to pick you up and embrace you. He's ready to dust you off and forgive your sins. His love for you goes so deep that heaven will rejoice when you decide to serve Him with all your heart.

Make that decision now. Believe with all your heart in who Christ is and repeat the prayer below with all your heart. Make every effort to get to know the Lord Jesus Christ on a personal level. Find a Bible teaching Holy Spirit-filled church close to your home and begin your new life in Christ. As you read this prayer, make it your own. Open your heart to Jesus Christ.

> *Heavenly Father, I know that I am a sinner. I recognize that you are the change that I need in my life. Jesus, I believe that you are the son of God and that you died for my sins. I also believe that you rose from the grave*

on the third day to set me free. Jesus, I ask you to come into my heart and be my Lord and Savior from this moment. I am saved, and I am covered with the precious blood of Jesus. Amen.

Congratulations, friend! The heavens are rejoicing at this very moment in your honor! Welcome to your new life in Christ. Nothing on earth will ever compare to the amazing love of Jesus.

LEANDRO OLIVAREZ

Chapter 16

Prayers

Prayers to help guide you in your daily walk with the Lord.

(Prayer of Repentance)

Father in heaven, In the name of Jesus Christ, I approach your Holy throne. Lord I ask for your mercy. I repent of my sins. (*name them if you can*). Wash me in the blood of Jesus. I accept your Son Jesus as my Savior, my Redeemer, my Refuge, and my Lord. Father, in heaven, forgive me of my every act of rebellion against you. I surrender to your will for me, for my life, my calling, and my family. I reject the works of the Devil. In the name of Christ Jesus, I pray. Amen.

> 2 Chronicles 7:14 - If my people, which are called by my name, shall humble themselves, and pray, and seek my face, and turn from their wicked ways; then will I hear from heaven, and will forgive their sin, and will heal their land.

(Prayer of Thanksgiving)

Heavenly Father, I come to you Lord. Thank you for your grace and mercy. Thank you for loving me and my family, and for giving me a second chance in life. You have been so good to me, Lord. I could never thank you enough with mere words. With thanksgiving, I will walk in obedience to your Word. Your grace is sufficient for me and my house. Thank you, Lord, for coming to my rescue. I was Lost, but now I am found. I love you, Lord. In the Name of Christ Jesus, I pray. Amen.

> Psalm 9:1 - I will give thanks to you, LORD, with all my heart; I will tell of all your wonderful deeds.

(Prayer for loved ones)

My Heavenly Father, Lord, I humbly ask for your hand of mercy over my loved ones. Please Lord accept my fasting for them. Lord, some of my loved ones believe in you. However, they don't serve you. They don't live for you, Lord. I am fasting and pleading with you, Lord, to show mercy and send someone they will listen to who will tell them about you. Have them, Lord, encounter one of your angels. Lord, please, spare my loved ones, I place them in your hands. In Jesus' name, I pray. Amen.

> Ezekiel 36:26 KJV - I will give you a new heart and put a new spirit within you; I will take the heart of stone out of your flesh and give you a heart of flesh.

(Prayer for your children)

Heavenly Father, please protect my children and open their understanding. I speak life and love and your peace over them. Father, place a hedge of protection around each of them. Lord Jesus, I claim your promises over my household. Walk with them everywhere they go and in everything they do. Lord, increase their spiritual discernment. In the name of Jesus Christ, I pray. Amen.

> Proverbs 2:6 - For the Lord giveth wisdom: out of his mouth cometh knowledge and understanding.

Take a few minutes to spend time with the Lord. Thank him for His goodness and mercy and know that He loves you and your family. Dedicate your family to the Lord and acknowledge Him in everything you do.

Please keep in mind that if the Lord wakes you up in the early morning hours, or late at night, even if it's to get a glass of water or use the restroom, it is not a coincidence. The Lord wants you to hear from you. Pray. Many times the Lord will alert us to pray. There may be a spiritual attack coming, or a loved one may be in danger. Remember, if you are on high alert spiritually the Lord will speak to you. Here are some spiritual warfare prayers that I pray, at all hours of the night and throughout the day. I begin every prayer with a prayer of repentance because our God is Holy, and we must reverence Him as the Holy God He is.

(Prayers before bedtime)

Heavenly Father, I submit myself to you. Speak to my spirit as you will. Father, forgive me for every sin, transgression, and all my trespasses. I repent of the iniquity in my bloodline, Lord. Send your warring angels to stand guard in my yard and in every room in my house, to stand guard over me and my family. Lord, if the enemy sends flaming arrows and tries to retaliate against me, commission your angels to intervene and stop the attack, and send it back with the same arrows dipped in your blood. Father, watch over us while we rest. In the name of Jesus Christ, I pray. Amen

> Proverbs 3:24 - When thou liest down, thou shalt not be afraid: yea, thou shalt lie down, and thy sleep shall be sweet.

(Prayers before I leave the house)

Father, in the mighty name of Jesus Christ, I dress myself in your righteousness, your complete armor. I cancel every demonic intention against me, my wife, and my children *(name them all)* against my job, and my ministry. I cancel every plan of the enemy, including every mental, emotional, financial attack, accident, injury, and premature death; and every attack against my church, and congregation. I break apart every demonic altar, and cancel every spoken word curse against my loved ones *(name them)* and I apply the living blood of Jesus over each one of them. Lord, walk with each of us today. In the name of Jesus Christ, I pray. Amen.

> Isaiah 54:17 - No weapon that is formed against thee shall prosper; and every tongue that shall rise against thee in judgment thou shalt condemn. This is the heritage of the servants of the LORD, and their righteousness is of me, saith the LORD.

Lord, I come against and bind any unclean spirits that are attacking my loved ones. In the mighty name of Jesus Christ I bind every spirit of depression, anxiety, rejection, fear, fear of rejection, self-rejection, and condemnation. Demonic spirits, I cancel your mission in the name of Jesus. I dismantle every demonic altar, every demonic contract, and I send confusion to the enemy's camp for them to destroy each other. In the name of Christ Jesus, my family and their minds are off limits to you Satan. In Christ Jesus' name I pray. Amen.

(A proclamation to defend your household)

Satan and every demon, I put you on notice right now in the mighty name of Jesus Christ. I command you to leave my home and my family *(name them)* right now. In the name of Jesus, I bind every foul demon of destruction, chaos, division and stagnation, every infirmity (weakness). I come against you in the name of the Lord Jesus Christ. I dismantle every demonic altar, and I burn every demonic contract with *(Name them here)*. I command you now in the name of Jesus Messiah, leave now. Amen.

> Matthew 4:10 KJV - Then saith Jesus unto him, get thee hence, (behind me) Satan: for it is written, thou shalt worship the Lord thy God, and him only shalt thou serve.

(Prayer to Cancel every spoken word curse)

Heavenly Father, I come before you in repentance. Forgive me Lord for every idle word that has ever come from my mouth against any of your servants, against you Lord, against my loved ones *(name them)*, against my spouse or my children. Lord, I repent of every spoken word curse over anyone and everyone including myself. I break every curse spoken, and every word of judgment spoken against me and my family *(name them)*. I break every demonic stronghold, and take back all authority I may have forfeited to the enemy. I strip the enemy of all legal rights now in the name of Jesus Christ. Father, I send back any curse thrown my way or towards my loved ones *(name them)*. I send those words back to torment those people until they repent to you, for what they have done. Lord, you have promised to fight my battles and to be with me in the fight. In the name of Jesus Christ, I pray. Amen.

> Isaiah 54:17 KJV - No weapon formed against you shall prosper, and every tongue which rises against you in judgment You shall condemn. This is the heritage of the servants of the LORD, and their righteousness is from Me," says the LORD.

(Proclamation against witchcraft)

Devil, and every demon that has come against me and my family, I come against you in the name of the Lord Jesus Christ! I put you on notice now that my family and I are covered in the atoning blood of Jesus. I cancel every demonic intention and assignment against me and my family *(name them)*. I burn with the fire of the Holy Spirit every demonic contract with my name or my family's name on it.

I cancel every mission, of attack, in the mighty name of Jesus Christ. I break every spoken word against me and my loved ones (name them) in the name of Jesus. The blood of Jesus has redeemed me and my family from your curse. I demolish and dismantle every demonic altar with my name and my family's name on it. I cancel every incantation, and every voodoo doll with my picture or name on it. I send the curse back to where it came from to carry out your assignment, until they surrender to God. As for me and my house, my bloodline, we will serve the Lord and you demons are never to return. Should you try to return the warring angels of heaven have been posted to decapitate you and send you bound to the feet of Jesus Christ, to await your punishment from the Almighty. I decree and declare this to go into motion now, in the name of Jesus. Amen.

(Prayer against sickness or disease)

Heavenly Father, I repent of all my sins, trespasses, transgression, and the iniquity in my bloodline. Father, your Word tells us that you have given us the authority to trample on snakes and scorpions and over all the power of the enemy. In your name, in the name of Christ Jesus, I come against this demon of *(Name your symptom)* and cancel and rebuke this spirit of, *(cancer, kidney problems, etc.)* I rip apart every demonic nest in my blood, in my mind, in my eyes, in my bones, in my organs, I dismantle every demonic nest of infirmity, sickness and disease. I apply the healing blood of Jesus Christ over every part of my body. Spirit of darkness, your assignment of death and torment over me is canceled now, in the name of Jesus Christ. Amen.

> Isaiah 53:5 - But he was wounded for our transgressions, he was bruised for our iniquities: the chastisement of our peace was upon him; and with his stripes, we are healed.

These are model prayers for you to pray over yourself, or for you to lay hands on someone to pray over them. But always remember to spend time with the Lord, in fasting, prayer, and worship. Always allow the Lord to guide you especially if the battle isn't yours to fight, but you are willing to help someone else in their fight. You must teach them that the word of God is our weapon of mass destruction against the enemy and is also our source of life. We must be dressed daily in the Lord's righteousness. If you give these prayers to someone, make sure you tell them that they must live a life of repentance, because if they try to war against the enemy without the blood covering of Jesus Christ, and the fire of the Holy Spirit, they will be worse off than before.

A relationship with the Father, the Son and the Holy Spirit is an absolute necessity; otherwise, they could end up like the seven sons of Sceva. These are people that want the power but don't want the Lord, and they completely misunderstand who Christ, and the Holy Spirit are. This is what happens when someone that does not have a personal relationship with the Lord tries to do battle in the name of the Lord.

What will happen is that those demons do not see Jesus Christ in them, and those demons can hurt them because there is no blood covering. Those demons do not see the Spirit of God in them, so please don't just go around telling people that don't want Jesus how to do this without them having a relationship with the Lord. Look at the scriptures. These sons of a priest named Sceva tried to "use the name of the one whom Paul preaches" the demons knew Jesus and they knew who Paul was but didn't see the Holy Spirit in these sons of Sceva the High Priest, check it out.

<u>Acts 19:13-16</u>

> 13) Then certain of the vagabond Jews, exorcists, took upon them to call over them which had evil spirits the name of the Lord Jesus, saying, we adjure you by Jesus whom Paul preacheth.
>
> 14) And there were seven sons of one Sceva, a Jew, and chief of the priests, which did so.
>
> 15) And the evil spirit answered and said, Jesus I know, and Paul I know; but who are ye?
>
> 16) And the man in whom the evil spirit was leaped on them, and overcame them, and prevailed against them, so that they fled out of that house naked and wounded.

If you have a relationship with Jesus Christ, you have the authority to do this, not just anyone can go into spiritual warfare without proper spiritual preparation. The name of Jesus Christ is not a magic formula. His name is our authority, and His blood is our protection, and His Word is our weapon.

Conclusion

As we have reached the end of this book, the main thing God wants to emphasize is the love that He has always had and still has for His people. He established His covenant with Abraham and to Abraham's seed, based on His love. God will show you His mercy, unwavering love, and His mighty power. However, we must apply his love to our daily walk in His righteousness.

The New Covenant through Christ is sealed in the blood of Jesus Christ for His Church. You must remember that the Church did not and will not replace Israel. Israel belongs to the Father (the Great nation; and many nations) belong to the Holy Spirit to gather His people to return to the Lord God Almighty. The (Holy Nation) is the Church that is the Bride of Christ. His never-ending love for His creation is true power. You will find this all in His promises to His people. May He bless you and guide your path. Come to Jesus and walk out your daily salvation.

Hebrews 8:7-12 KJV

7) For if that first covenant had been faultless, then should no place have been sought for the second.

8) For finding fault with them, he saith, Behold, the days come, saith the Lord, when I will make a new covenant with the house of Israel and with the house of Judah:

9) Not according to the covenant that I made with their fathers in the day when I took them by the hand to lead them out of the land of Egypt; because they continued not in my covenant, and I regarded them not, saith the Lord.

10) For this is the covenant that I will make with the house of Israel after those days, saith the Lord; I will put my laws into their mind, and write them in their hearts: and I will be to them a God, and they shall be to me a people:

11) And they shall not teach every man his neighbor, and every man his brother, saying, Know the Lord: for all shall know me, from the least to the greatest.

12) For I will be merciful to their unrighteousness, and their sins and their iniquities will I remember no more.

Blessings,

Pastor Lenn Olivarez